The Joan Palevsky  Imprint in Classical Literature

In honor of beloved Virgil—

"O degli altri poeti onore e lume . . ."

—Dante, *Inferno*

The publisher gratefully acknowledges the generous contribution to this book provided by the Classical Literature Endowment Fund of the University of California Press Foundation, which is supported by a major gift from Joan Palevsky.

The Economy of the Greek Cities

The Economy of the Greek Cities

*From the Archaic Period
to the Early Roman Empire*

Léopold Migeotte

Translated by Janet Lloyd

UNIVERSITY OF CALIFORNIA PRESS

Berkeley   Los Angeles   London

University of California Press, one of the most distinguished university presses in the United States, enriches lives around the world by advancing scholarship in the humanities, social sciences, and natural sciences. Its activities are supported by the UC Press Foundation and by philanthropic contributions from individuals and institutions. For more information, visit www.ucpress.edu.

Title of the original French edition: *L'économie des cités grecques*. Published by Ellipses, copyright 2002 Édition Marketing S.A.

University of California Press
Berkeley and Los Angeles, California

University of California Press, Ltd.
London, England

Library of Congress Cataloging-in-Publication Data

Migeotte, Léopold.

[Economie des cités grecques. English]   The economy of the Greek cities : from the archaic period to the early Roman Empire / Léopold Migeotte ; translated by Janet Lloyd.

    p.   cm.

Includes bibliographical references and index.
ISBN 978-0-520-25365-0 (cloth, alk. paper)
ISBN 978-0-520-25366-7 (pbk., alk. paper)
1. Greece—Economic conditions—To 146 B.C.   I. Title.

HC37.M5413   2009
330.938—dc22   2008050892

Manufactured in the United States of America

18   17   16   15   14   13   12   11   10   09
10   9   8   7   6   5   4   3   2   1

The paper used in this publication meets the minimum requirements of ANSI/NISO Z39.48-1992 (R 1997) (*Permanence of Paper*).

CONTENTS

FOREWORD

The first edition of the present work (Paris, 2002) has already been translated into Italian (Rome, Carocci, 2003) and Modern Greek (Athens, Papadimas, 2007). Both translations have been revised by the author, who provided the translators with a fair number of modifications and supplementary bibliographical references. The present English translation is based on the text of the second French edition (Paris, 2007), which incorporates not only the improvements made to the two earlier translations but also a number of new passages. Furthermore, as explained in the introduction, in accordance with the limits of what proves useful, the bibliography has been brought up to date and adapted for an English-speaking public.

Map 1. The Aegean world

Map 2. The eastern Mediterranean and the Black Sea

Map 3. The western Mediterranean

Introduction

THE PURPOSE AND NATURE OF THIS BOOK

The study of the economy of the ancient world has been much reinvigorated and enriched over the last few decades. There have been many detailed research studies into realia and these have provided precious information, despite their non-theoretical nature, which in many cases limits them to observation and description. At the other end of the spectrum, studies have tackled the subject from a wider perspective, seeking to produce a new, overall, and abstract analysis of certain fundamental features of the ancient economy. The latter studies tend to be inspired by anthropological and economic models. In an innovative and sometimes stimulating fashion, they illuminate a number of aspects of the economic domain but do so at the cost of a some- what reductionist effect, all too often freezing the past in a frame that reflects only one particular period or a limited part of the subject. There have also, happily, been quite a few studies that have brought new viewpoints to bear upon already familiar texts and either old or new archaeological data, deploying innovative methods that are mentioned below in my description of the sources I have used. It is also chiefly this third category of studies that has encouraged researchers to look afresh and critically at long-accepted ideas and dominant doctrines relating to the economy of the ancient world.

Much of this research work is marked by fundamental old debates that need to be briefly summarized here. The earliest controversy dates back to the nineteenth century, when "Modernists" clashed with "Primitivists." The Modernists, impressed by the dynamism of ancient craft industries and trade, described the ancient economy in modern terms, discerning between it and the economy of today differences not of nature but only of degree, as M. Rostovtseff, the most illustrious representative of this trend, put it. In contrast, the Primitivists, who frequently referred to the so-called primitive societies studied by anthropologists, considered the ancient world to have been static and set in its ways and to have practiced a rural subsistence economy in which trade played no significant role. M. I. Finley is considered the most typical representative of this trend, but the positions he adopts have sometimes been crudely caricatured: for example, he expressed certain reservations regarding the relevance, for Greek society, of models borrowed from civilizations without writing. The second controversy, which bore certain affinities to the first and which has frequently been confused with it, was between "Formalists" and "Substantivists." The former, convinced that the science of economics had correctly identified the universal principles of economic rationality, sought to apply these to the study of the ancient economy, which they considered to be an autonomous sphere, certainly less developed than the economy of today, but comparable to it. The latter argued that this method, founded on the study of a market economy, was unsuited to an analysis of ancient economies, which were fundamentally different. In the 1950s, K. Polanyi vigorously defended in particular the idea that the Greek economy should only be studied within the framework of its own institutions, for it was "embedded" in all the networks and constraints of society as a whole. This fruitful idea provided much inspiration for M.I. Finley, who drew from it excellent conclusions concerning, for example, the role that social status played in economic behavior. In truth, it was an idea that, mutatis mutandis, could be applied to any economy, even that of the present day; for, contrary to theories according to which the domain of economics is an abstract entity that may be expressed in mathematical formulae, modes of production, exchange, and consumption are always influenced by their political, social, and cultural context. However that may be, for several decades research was dominated by the thinking of Finley, now described as "neo-primitivism," now as "the new orthodoxy." A number of recent studies have questioned it and tried to reach beyond it. The debate has thus moved into a whole new phase, which is all to the good. As a result, however, where many still controversial subjects are concerned, syntheses can be no more than provisional.

The present work is designed to be both accessible to students new to the field and also concise. On the assumption that its readers will possess only an elementary knowledge of ancient history, it aims to constitute no more than an introduction: it avoids the finer points of erudite discussion and presents brief, up-to-date analyses of general questions. It is certainly based on a number of detailed readings, but so as to keep the text uncluttered, it does not refer systematically to them all. That is why only references to ancient texts are indicated. (They are, on the one hand, to authors whose works are easily available in translation, on the other to collections of translated texts whose titles are indicated at the beginning of the bibliography at the end of this volume.) Similarly, in the bibliography, utility has prevailed over exhaustiveness: the supplementary reading list has been compiled from mostly recent studies, most of them published in English.

Proceeding from a simple definition of the economy, this book describes activities involving the production, exchange, and consumption of material goods and services in the Greek cities of antiquity. To be precise, it strives to show how these activities interacted and operated within the political, social, and cultural context. In order to maintain a unified point of view, this inquiry concentrates on the Greek cities. To be sure, it takes into account their relations with the larger states that took them over; but, owing to limitations of space, it has not been possible to devote even one or two chapters to the latter, in particular the Hellenistic kingdoms. Of course, it would have been possible to limit the present analysis to one particular well-known city or group of cities. However, it seemed important to cover the Greek world as a whole, despite the double challenge of dealing with so large an area and so long a period of time.

The world of the Greek cities went through several phases of expansion and eventually covered a vast area: it extended far beyond the Aegean world to many of the shores of the Mediterranean and the Black Sea and, subsequently, also to the interior of Asia Minor and ultimately, in an even more dispersed fashion, to the heart of the Middle East and the frontiers of India. It was thus a world of great diversity. The number of its cities, some of them very small, has been estimated at over one thousand in the classical period, and later (according to literary evidence) at as many as fifteen hundred. But what is most striking is that, with few exceptions, wherever they settled, the Greeks reproduced the model with which they were familiar and which they considered to be that of civilized men, namely the *polis,* a city or city-state complete with the particular urban framework and institutions that had taken shape in Greece. In the economic domain, in particular, there were many similarities in technical and material conditions and also in many practices and attitudes. Thus it is possible to pick out certain characteristics shared in common throughout this world without reducing them to a homogenizing typology.

Moreover, it is by now increasingly accepted that these cities remained the major frameworks of Greek life for over a thousand years. It is generally agreed that the *polis,* with all its characteristics, began to become established in the eighth century B.C. Admittedly, this involved a long and complex process, which took longer in some places than in others. But the outstanding fact is that, as early as the archaic period (roughly 800–500 B.C.), the city was everywhere considered to be the motherland of a Greek citizen and the normal center of his life; and this model became increasingly firmly established in the classical period (roughly 500–325 B.C.) and then continued to spread, not only in the Hellenistic period (roughly 325–30 B.C.), but also under the early Roman Empire (roughly 30 B.C. to the end of the second century A.D.) and even thereafter. To be sure, over the centuries cities underwent important changes. In the first place, they were progressively absorbed into greater units governed by central authorities (first the Hellenistic kingdoms, then the Roman Empire), which eventually imposed political unity upon them. Secondly, from the second century B.C. onward, their internal politics increasingly became dominated by oligarchies of "notables" (prominent citizens). Some even reformed their institutions with a view to encouraging this. It has often been suggested that it was as a result of this that they ceased to be significant independent entities. This is not the place to return to that debate, the economic aspects of which are tackled in chapter 1. But it is worth pointing out, in the wake of M. Rostovtseff, L. Robert, and P. Gauthier, that this did not cause the cities either to disappear or to be drained of their political substance. The present inquiry therefore covers an extremely long period. In such a short book, it is clearly not possible to present a relatively continuous history of the Greek economy in all its diversity. Nevertheless, despite all the changes, we will be struck by the long continuities in economic conditions, practices, and attitudes.

As to methodology, this handbook tries to bypass controversies; it attempts above all to make full use of both the ancient sources and the advances achieved by the latest research and to bring all these to bear upon major questions. In so doing, it draws upon a number of explanatory models in precise contexts. It does not, however, start out with any particular model or theory in mind since, by definition, abstract arguments that remain at the level of generalities cannot really illuminate the evolution and diversity of the past. On the other hand, given that any historical inquiry is inevitably bound to use modern concepts and vocabulary, comparisons with our own ways of behaving and thinking today are sometimes drawn; but they neither serve as points of reference nor provide a basis for value judgments concerning the Greeks, either positive or negative. Admittedly, it was tempting to establish parallels with the towns of the later Middle Ages in the West, which have often been compared to the Greek cities. But when analyzed, such comparisons proved unfruitful since, over and above a few similarities, numerous differences remained. The Greek cities truly were unique centers of life. Their economic activities and attitudes therefore needed to be set within their own particular framework and, as far as possible, interpreted in the light of analyses produced by the Greeks themselves, always, of course, taking into account their own particular points of view and the context in which these were formed.

The pages that follow use both synchronic and diachronic analyses. Chapter 1 describes both the constant and the evolving structural features that provided the framework for the economy of the cities. The three chapters that follow are, in traditional fashion, devoted to agriculture, craft industries, and trade, respectively, and seek to identify the dominant characteristics and major tendencies in each. This is, of course, an artificial division, since the three domains were closely interconnected and all evolved together. Nevertheless, it does make for clarity.

SOURCES

All studies of antiquity are bound to face the problem of lost sources, first and foremost that of written documents.

From Orality to Writing

At the dawn of the archaic period, the Greeks knew nothing of writing. It is true that between the fifteenth and the twelfth century B.C., the rulers of the Mycenaean palaces had used a syllabic system to make their inventories; but that technique was later lost, and it was not until the eighth century (at the latest) that the Greeks adapted an alphabet inspired by the Phoenicians to write their own language. This appropriation may have taken place within circles of merchants who were in contact with the Near East, after which this new tool was diffused more widely along the trading routes. However, the earliest texts preserved from this period have nothing to do with the economy. In this domain and others too, the habits of orality persisted for centuries. Daily agricultural and crafts production and local bartering transactions functioned well enough without writing. Even where more far-flung trading was concerned, agreements and contracts were effected orally, before witnesses, and in some cases were backed by oaths. In this way they acquired legal validity.

Furthermore, very few echoes of economic activities are to be found in the literary sources. For the archaic period, we find only scattered allusions in the various poetic works and in Hesiod's poem *Works and Days,* which evokes rural life in Boeotia around 700 B.C. Fortunately, we possess from the classical period the two dialogues of Xenophon's Oeconomicus and also his *Poroi,* a short work devoted to Athenian finances in the mid-fourth century. But while Greek intellectuals do thus evoke and analyze a number of aspects of their economy, they neither theorized about it nor studied its history. Hence, as for subsequent ones, we need to turn to many different kinds of works: historical, geographical, philosophical, rhetorical, dramatic, medical, and botanical, works such as the *Histories* of Herodotus and Polybius, the comedies of Aristophanes and Menander, Plato's *Laws,* Aristotle's *Politics,* the speeches of the Athenian orators, the essays of the Hippocratic writers, Theophrastus, Plutarch, and so forth. These texts need to be read with particularly critical attention, because in many cases they reflect not reality itself but their authors' own representations of it. Moreover, most of the texts from the classical period come from Athens and so tell us little about other cities, the smaller ones in particular.

All the same, writing must have become accepted relatively early in economic circles, where particularly delicate or complex operations were concerned, both among private individuals and within the public administration. By bestowing a fixed and durable form upon all kinds of documents (contracts, leases, commercial agreements and credit notes, records of manumissions, laws, regulations, accounts and inventories . . .), writing made it possible not only to create archives but also to produce evidence in the event of disputes. A scene depicting the taking of an inventory is represented on a Laconian cup dating from the mid-sixth century B.C. It shows Arcesilaus, the king of Cyrene, and eight of his staff engaged in weighing, recording, and storing (or loading on to a ship?) tubers of silphion (a local plant used both as a medicament and as a condiment, which contributed to Cyrene's wealth). In Corcyra, around 500, acknowledgments of debts were recorded by being engraved on lead tablets. We also possess commercial correspondence, likewise inscribed on lead tablets, from the late sixth (or possibly the fifth) century. By a few years later, anyone who, like Pericles, kept strict accounts for his *oikos* (see below, p. 86) must have resorted to writing. The same clearly applies to the incumbent administrations of cities and sanctuaries and to banks, which produced *trapezitika grammata* that are recorded in fourth-century Athenian sources. In this same period, Aristotle (*Politics* 1338a15–17) noted the usefulness of writing (*ta grammata*) not only for study and politics, but also in the business world (*chrēmatismos*) and in the running of a household (*oikonomia*). It was in Athens, precisely in a commercial context, that the adoption of written contracts (*syngraphai*) is attested in the second half of the fourth century, initially no doubt for business deals that involved large sums of money and that were particularly risky: for example, the transport of goods and loans on bottomry for ships engaged in distant trading ventures, loans of money to wholesalers or shipowners, particularly where maritime trading was involved. All the same, writing did not eliminate the old custom of depending on witnesses: their legal depositions continued to be valued, alongside written contracts. In fact, a copy of the contract would sometimes be entrusted to one of the witnesses.

Most of the original texts have disappeared, as they were written on perishable materials: wax or wooden tablets, rolls of papyrus, or animal skins, none of which, clearly, have survived—at any rate not in the world of the Greek cities. Fortunately though, from the archaic and above all the classical periods onward, the Greeks took to engraving copies of such documents on durable materials such as stone or, sometimes, bronze, so that they might be seen more widely and would last longer. The public domain benefited from this more than the private did, and the Hellenistic period is better represented by such sources than others. The most useful documents are the inventories and accounts sheets from sanctuaries and cities, the agreements and treaties between states, and the records of legislative and juridical measures relating to economic or fiscal matters: traces of these have come down to us from the archaic period and above all from the fifth century B.C. onward. We are thus in possession of a considerable, albeit widely dispersed, harvest of documentation, which continues to increase thanks to archaeological excavations and chance discoveries. Texts such as these possess two advantages over literary sources: they put us in direct contact with the realities of the period and make it possible to break away from Athenocentricity, since from the fifth century onward, in particular, they originate in many other cities and regions, some of them remote. All the same, they are not entirely representative, for the choice of which texts to engrave was in many cases influenced by their honorific or spectacular nature. Routine, day-to-day documents, whether public or private, were not necessarily accorded such privileged treatment.

Archaeology and Numismatics

Archaeology has won a new lease on life by embracing material culture in its entirety and by diversifying its methods. To be sure, excavations continue, and monumental remains, necropolises, tools, weapons, and ceramics (in particular those bearing pictorial representations), individual coins, and monetary hoards all continue to shed light on the ancient Greek economy and daily life. Now, however, attention is paid to all excavated material, not just to selected decorated or inscribed objects. Increasingly, terrains are carefully surveyed, aerial and satellite photography are used, along with ecology, geography, and geology, while models of spatial organization help researchers to study populations, the organization of the rural world, the layout and density of settlements, the positioning of units of production such as metallurgical and ceramic kilns, routes of communication, and the layout and size of certain infrastructures such as ports and public squares, among others. Studies of the countryside, in particular, have been positively revolutionized. Underwater excavations now take place so that wrecks and their cargoes can be studied. On top of all this, techniques are borrowed from the exact sciences: the electromagnetic surveying of sites, the dating of objects by carbon 14 or thermoluminescence, the physicochemical analysis of pollens, seeds, and remains of vegetation, and of geological formations. All are techniques that can throw light upon agricultural life, the environment, and foodstuffs. Studies of metals, ceramics, and marble sometimes reveal the composition and origins of those materials; palaeopathology (the study of skeletons and bones) yields information about the health and age of the deceased and even, in the case of women, the number of children they have borne. However, as in the case of inscriptions, such evidence is not entirely unbiased, since only nonperishable materials and objects have survived: metal tools but not wooden ones, amphoras but not their contents, the remains of workshops but not their equipment, and so on.

Numismatics merits particular attention, by reason of the abundance of material and the refinement of research methods. Neutronically activated analyses, metrology applied to different series of coins, and analyses of mints and their modes of stamping reveal with increasing precision the quality and provenance of the metals, the intensity and rhythms of minting, the degree of dispersion of the minted coins, and the duration of their circulation: all phenomena that are clearly linked to the economic activities of both states and private individuals.

There is thus no shortage of new information. Some ceramic and monetary series, such as stamped amphoras, can even provide the bases for statistical analyses or become the subject of computerized studies. But overall, sources are still too rare, too lacunose, and too dispersed. Attempts at quantification, always popular in economic studies, in general remain impossible or unreliable, although such drawbacks are less severe in the case of the Hellenistic period. In the last analysis, the combination of many types of sources does make it possible to arrive at satisfactory generalizations, to qualify them to some extent, and not to lend too much weight to the example provided by Athens.

The Greek Cities
and the Economy

This chapter presents a broad outline of the material, mental, and institutional context within which the economy of Greek cities developed. It constitutes a basis for the three chapters that follow it and introduces a number of questions that they will pursue and study more closely.

CONSTANTS AND CONSTRAINTS
The Geographical Setting

Except for the cities established at the heart of Asia Minor and in the Middle East, natural conditions were essentially similar, give or take a few variants, throughout the Greek world. Those conditions were certainly harsher and more unyielding than can be imagined by today's tourists and vacationers. As the historian Herodotus wrote in the fifth century B.C. (VII.102), "In Hellas poverty is ever native to the soil, but courage comes of [one's] own seeking, the fruit of wisdom and strong law" (translated by A.D. Godley, The Loeb Classical Library, 1950).

Despite a gradual rise in sea levels, which has altered the details of some of its coasts, the topography of the Mediterranean is still as it was 2,500 years ago. Geologically speaking, the land is young, and it is therefore unstable. A number of volcanoes are still active, and earthquakes are relatively frequent. Mountains occupy at least 80 percent of the Greek lands, in the Mediterranean area at any rate, and more than 90 percent in the small islands of the Aegean. The many barriers they form certainly affected the creation of new cities. From an economic point of view, these mountains limit the number and size of the plains and plateaus suited to agriculture and stock-raising, and they also complicate and impede travel and transport. The land offers a variety of possibilities for agriculture, stock-raising, hunting, and forestry, but on the whole it is rocky, and its productivity is mediocre. Several studies have shown that the forests of pines, oaks, beeches, and chestnut trees used to be more numerous and more dense than they are today. But as early as the archaic period they were probably giving way to agriculture, heaths, and scrubland. In the classical period their coppices and bushes still provided enough firewood and material for charcoal but no longer supplied enough for the construction of buildings or ships. The effects of agriculture are controversial. Some believe that it progressively exhausted and eroded the soil. But in truth intensive use and care of the land, particularly terracing, seem to be the best ways to preserve it. The land also provided some excellent clay, an abundance of stone and, in particular, fine marble. Mineral resources varied from one place to another: there were many seams of iron; a little copper, which was mixed with tin imported from afar to create objects of bronze; and, most important, the gold and silver of several mines were used in making precious objects and coins.

The sea was never far away, at least in the Mediterranean area and the Black Sea region. In fact, the Greeks preferred to settle along the coasts or not far from them, and even cities further inland generally enjoyed access to a port not far distant. Thanks to the many sheltered coves and landmarks offered by the indented coastline and the islands, particularly those in the Aegean, the Greeks made the sea their "royal road" for the purposes of communication. Moreover, the sea not only created salt-flats but provided ample fishing stocks that were exploited wherever possible.

Many Greek poets and learned men have sung the praises of their well-balanced climate; and since most Greeks lived in a Mediterranean climate, we may disregard the continental zones of Asia Minor and the Middle East. The Greek climate was characterized by two sharply contrasted seasons, as it still is today. By April the spring begins to herald the heat and aridity of summer. The end of September sees the return of rains, sometimes torrential, and cold. The cold increases as the months pass, but, except in the mountainous regions, with their ice and snow it is never really bitter. Outdoor life, universally adopted in the summer, is now much reduced. But most important for agriculture and stock-raising is the rainy season, which is indispensable both for vegetation and for replenishing the wells, cisterns, and reservoirs with stores of water. The rains are borne in by westerly winds in the course of the winter and spring, varying greatly from one place to another, sometimes even over short distances. While the north and northwest of mainland Greece, the shores of the Black Sea, and several parts of Asia Minor are relatively well watered, Attica, the Cyclades, the southern Peloponnese, and Crete remain far more arid. Except in the mountains, most of the watercourses, which are filled by the winter rains, dry up in the summer. The fresh water of rivers, lakes, and springs is therefore scarce and very precious.

The Level of Technology

Ancient tool-production was extremely conservative. The Primitivist school of thought attributed its lack of innovation to certain mental attitudes that may have blocked technical development, such as the Greeks' respect for the natural order, their disdain for craft industries, a divorce between theory and practice, and the absence of a spirit of enterprise or any notion of progress. As the three chapters that follow will show, some of their arguments do contain a degree of truth. In the Bronze Age, the Greeks borrowed from Egypt and the Near East many techniques that they then adapted to their own needs and preserved for centuries. By the archaic period, many tools and items of equipment had already been in use for a long time, some ever since the Neolithic period: sickles, plows, mattocks, two-pronged hoes, mills, presses, potter's wheels and kilns, distaffs, looms, a variety of hand tools, and so on. Bronze metallurgy dated from the third millennium, iron metallurgy from the end of the second. Manpower and animal power had always been the principal sources of energy. However, the problem is more complex than it may appear.

Recent research, based mostly on archaeology, has shown that many pieces of equipment continued to be adapted and improved

from one generation to another, in most cases by the users themselves in a trial-and-error fashion. For instance, after the year
1000, iron metallurgy progressively spread, producing more
effective tools, particularly for minting and engraving. When, in
the eighth century B.C., long-distance relations were resumed,
bronze metallurgy reappeared and was employed for the
weaponry of footsoldiers in particular. By the sixth century, glass
technology was known, and between the sixth and fourth centuries potters managed to achieve excellent glazes by controlling
firing temperatures. Navigation techniques for sea voyages,
involving the square sail and oars, with two steering oars at the
stern (instead of a sternpost rudder), adequately served the needs
of the day. On land, harnessing equipment was more efficient
than has sometimes been claimed. Horses tended to be used as
mounts rather than as draft animals. While donkeys or mules
usually carried light loads, oxen pulled heavier ones. As early as
the archaic period, harnessing equipment made it possible to
move such considerable loads as logs of wood and blocks of stone
for building: a spectacular example is provided by the hauling of
goods and boats across a number of isthmuses that were used as
shortcuts, in particular the famous Corinth *Diolkos*. Derricks,
pulleys, winches, and hoists were used to raise heavy burdens;
and assembling such equipment required accurate measuring
tools. In the domain of agriculture, although farming tools
evolved very little, processing techniques did make considerable
progress. The manual mortars, mills, and grinders that had long
been used to mill grain were first replaced by a grinding mill
with a hopper and a to-and-fro movement (known as the
Olynthus grinding mill), which began to be diffused in the fifth
century. Improved in a few isolated attempts, this was replaced

in the first century B.C. by a rotary mill operated either by man-power or by animals. This was also used to grind mineral ores. Mills operated by a vertical wheel appeared in the second century A.D. Similarly, a number of mills with grinders for crushing olives are attested in the fourth century B.C. Increasingly effective olive presses were introduced, ranging from the levered press of the archaic period to the screw-press of the late Hellenistic period. The Greeks had always used large ceramic jars (*pithoi*) to store grain, but they also constructed granaries. We should also note the techniques employed for the extraction and processing of minerals, for the conveyance of water, for irrigation, and for drainage (wells, surface ditches, and underground canals such as Eupalinus's famous tunnel on the island of Samos, as early as the sixth century), as well as water clocks and the Archimedes screw, which was diffused from the Hellenistic period onward, and so on. The use of artificial incubators, mentioned by Aristotle as an Egyptian invention, was common in the same period.

All this testifies indisputably to a complex and inventive expertise. Such progress remained cautious, however, and antiquity did not produce any revolution in this domain. All the same, this conservative tendency should not be judged by the yardstick of the technological ferment of the modern world. The Greek world was governed by the natural constraints and resources of the time. It had its own particular needs, ways of functioning, and logic. As in most societies of the past, farmers and craftsmen generally remained faithful to the tools and techniques that had proved to be effective for generations. Routine was the rule, and the diffusion of innovations was slow. For example, the rotary mill, known in Spain as early as the late sixth century B.C., took four or five centuries to spread, in a variety of forms, throughout the Mediterranean. The level of technology could thus vary greatly from one region to another.

Demography and Health

Without doubt European Greece experienced strong demographic growth in the eighth century B.C. Precise figures cannot certainly be given, however, and the population may have started to increase earlier. In any case, the phenomenon was significant, with repercussions in the expansion and density of settlements, the emergence of cities, and the organization of labor. It produced, moreover, a strong wave of emigration that lasted for six generations, from the mid-eighth century to the mid-sixth. In the fifth century B.C. (still in European Greece), the population appears to have peaked at three million inhabitants—a conjectural figure but one certainly greater than that for more recent periods. Density, varying considerably from one region to another, has been the subject of many debates. While the island of Aegina had about two hundred inhabitants per square kilometer, Attica had one hundred, Boeotia and Megaris fewer than one hundred, and other places—such as Laconia, Messenia, Euboea, and a number of mountainous regions in central and western Greece (Phocis, Locris, Aetolia, Acarnania)—were far less densely populated. The populations of northern Greece and Macedonia peaked in the following century. Including other Mediterranean and Eastern cities, for which we possess very little information, the Greek world as a whole may have been home to between eight and ten million inhabitants in the second half of the fourth century.

Following the relative calm of the classical period, a significant migratory movement began when Egypt and the East were opened up as a result of Alexander the Great's conquests between 334 and 323 B.C. and the possibilities offered by the Seleucid kingdom in particular. The creation of new cities, above all in Asia Minor, testifies to continuing movement throughout the third century B.C. The scale of this migratory movement is impossible to evaluate, but it clearly decreased the population of a number of regions in mainland Greece. From the second half of the second century onward, these regions and the Aegean islands became embroiled in the tumult of various political events. (See the next section of this chapter.) Archaeological surveys confirm the demographic decline, which is deplored in various literary sources (Polybius XXXVI.17 and Dio Chrysostom VII.34). (See below, p. 84.)

Asia Minor, in contrast, seems not to have been affected. Furthermore, in the course of the Hellenistic period, under the influence of the Greek model, a number of native communities gradually came to adopt Greek language and customs. When they also took over Greek institutions, they were in a position to accede to the status of cities, with the support and protection of kings. Under the early Roman Empire this process of Hellenization continued, reaching as far afield as the Euphrates, where the eastern frontier of the empire was finally drawn. In the second century A.D. and even the third, under the Severan emperors, the expansion of cities and Greek-speaking populations reached its peak. As L. Robert puts it, this expansion represented the climax of Hellenization under the aegis of Rome.

Until at least the third century B.C., demographic growth seems to have remained fairly constant in European Greece, despite the effects of high infant mortality and the use of certain means of birth control. A number of epigraphical studies show that a family may have had, on average, four children. Some palaeopathological analyses even indicate that fertile women may have given birth to five or six children, though only about 2.5 per family survived. Life expectancy seems to have peaked in the fifth century but is extremely difficult to evaluate. It appears to have been less than forty years for women, as a result of poor nutrition and mortality in childbirth, but was slightly higher for men, a few of whom survived into old age. The demographic balance was always precarious. On the one hand, agriculture demanded a sufficient level of manpower but was unable to feed too large a population without resorting to imports. On the other hand, too pronounced a fall in population numbers spelled decline.

Palaeopathological analyses reveal that in the eighth century health conditions improved, with a diet increasingly rich in cereals, and life expectancy increased. At this point conditions appear to have been relatively good: on the whole the environment was healthy; food, though not abundant, was in sufficient and balanced supply; conditions of hygiene were satisfactory; and medicine made considerable progress, particularly from the classical period onward, under the influence of the Hippocratic and other medical schools. The Greek world did not suffer any major epidemics such as the Black Death, leprosy, or smallpox. All the same, the powers of medicine were limited, and fevers and intestinal and pulmonary afflictions persisted. Some research studies have even detected traces of malnutrition in a number of poverty-stricken strata of the population, especially among women and children.

Violence and Insecurity

Over the centuries a number of disruptive elements inflicted varying degrees of damage upon the economy. The most harmful was warfare, the negative effects of which are well known: loss of life, material destruction, insecurity, and the disruption of production and trade. If the impact of this was variable, losses of human life in general took longer to repair than material destruction. The conflicts of the classical period, between coalitions of cities, occurred on an unprecedented scale and resulted in considerable damage, both human and material, at least in some regions, such as the Peloponnese, and in cities such as Sparta. These wars were among the causes of the social disruption in the centuries that followed. (See below, p. 44.) In every period, local conflicts between cities and (in the fourth century and later, in the Hellenistic period) major clashes between royal powers could be lethal and lead to disaster, locally at least, in particular when plantations and harvests were systematically devastated and, above all, when towns were destroyed and their inhabitants were driven from their homes or sold as slaves. In the second half of the Hellenistic period, conflicts between Rome and the kings, followed by the wars against Mithridates and the civil wars between Roman generals in the first century, proved catastrophic. Massacres, destruction, deportations, the sacking of towns and sanctuaries, the armies' demands, the exactions of numerous Roman merchants, and the greed of publicans (Roman tax farmers) all combined to ruin a number of cities and even to depopulate certain regions. (See below, p. 84.) With the advent of the empire, the *pax Romana* was gradually imposed, and small local conflicts slowly disappeared. Augustus and several of his successors expended much effort and money to remedy the situation and restore prosperity. Mainland Greece and the Aegean islands, however, unlike Asia Minor, never recovered completely.

For a long time the seas were infested by piracy, except where cities or kings suppressed or controlled it. Piracy even acquired a kind of legitimacy, like that of warfare. Plato (*Laws* VII.823b–e) and Aristotle (*Politics* 1256a35–40 and 1256b23–26) classified both war and piracy together with hunting. In its own way, piracy played a commercial role, for pirates' plunder found its way to ports that derived profit from it, and those who had been robbed, particularly if they were freemen, often bought it back. Regions such as Aetolia and Crete, where this predatory mind-set persisted, openly practiced piracy, particularly in the Hellenistic period, and would enter into negotiations with other cities that were seeking safeguards and protection. When states at war integrated piracy into their conflicts, piracy itself turned into running warfare. Powerful cities such as Athens and Rhodes tried to combat piracy, considering it both harmful and unlawful. But in the end only the power of Rome managed to reduce it throughout the Mediterranean, under Pompey's aegis in 67 B.C. Wreckers also practiced a kind of piracy, but this seems to have persisted only among non-Greek peoples, as did legal rights to the contents of vessels that were wrecked (an ever-present risk in seafaring).

Banditry, about which much less is known, was certainly not as all-pervasive as piracy, but in many regions it was an ongoing scourge, despite all efforts at repression and control. It flourished above all in times of unrest and always inflicted grave damage upon trade on land, agriculture, and the craft industries.

The Greeks recognized various legitimate forms of seizure (*sylān*), the right to mulct an individual of his possessions (or one of his possessions) to compensate for some wrong he had done. In the cities, as early as the archaic period, litigation between private individuals would be handled by judges. Mutual agreements drawn up between neighboring cities with frequent contacts progressively defined the procedures to be followed in the courts. (See below, p. 154.) But in more distant cities linked by no such agreements, the right of seizure continued to apply. If the grievance involved private individuals, it seems (though this is not certain) that in principle the injured party, in person, would be obliged to have it out with whoever had wronged him, but in practice, for want of other recourse, he would turn for support to a relative, someone close to him, or some fellow citizen whom he considered to be affected by the wrong. An act of seizure, although violent, since it encountered resistance, was nevertheless not arbitrary, for it represented a form of justice, abided by certain rules, and was carried out in the presence of witnesses. As time passed, however, and the circulation of goods, men, and ideas increased, the right of seizure was gradually replaced by other procedures (see below, p. 154), although it did not disappear altogether. It continued to be observed when the grievance was of a public nature, in particular (as several Hellenistic inscriptions testify) when a city was slow to settle its debts. In such a case every citizen, and even that city's metics (resident foreigners), became involved. At the end of the third century B.C., just such a misfortune befell a metic domiciled in Delphi, the city having fallen into debt and its creditor having no doubt exhausted the usual formal procedures to extract repayment. Probably while this metic was visiting the city of the creditor (or traveling in its vicinity), his possessions were seized "in the name of the city." Upon his return to Delphi, he demanded compensation and received it, in the form of a tax exemption (L. Migeotte, *L'emprunt public,* no. 30).

It is not hard to see how such seizures (or the threat of them) might disrupt trade, for example by forcing merchants to avoid certain locations. As in other periods and other places, insecurity and danger were no doubt part of daily life. But we should not suppose either that the world of Greek antiquity was a savage one or that its cities were closed environments where foreigners possessed no rights. As we shall see (pp. 152–54), there were many different means of protecting trade and offering reassurance to traders. Furthermore, even though warfare was endemic right down to the beginning of the Roman period, peace was the normal state, and many cities, in particular the smaller ones, enjoyed long periods of calm. Finally, it is worth noting that from an economic point of view warfare could produce positive as well as negative effects; Aristotle considered it to be, in a way, a natural mode of acquisition (*Politics* 1256b23–26). In the first place, it was a source of profit for the victor: booty (in the form of both men and goods), new territories, indemnities imposed upon the vanquished, and so on. And, more generally, it stimulated productivity and trade in arms and whatever was needed to equip and provision the troops, and also in building materials, and so on. Furthermore, warfare frequently occasioned the minting of new coins. The matter is thus a complex one, even though ultimately the disadvantages certainly outweighed the advantages.

ECONOMY AND *OIKONOMIA*
The Economy and Work

In their daily lives, the Greeks were clearly aware of the economic realities of their time. They knew that their well-being and that of their city depended on production and trade. They were also capable of naming and describing the entire range of such activities. But they had no generic term equivalent to our "economy" to designate them as a whole. To be sure, from the classical period onward they frequently used *oikonomia,* from which the modern term is derived. However, this word had a private sense and primarily designated the management of an *oikos,* the basic unit in agricultural production, consisting of one family, in a wider sense that included its slaves and material possessions. Later, in the last quarter of the fourth century B.C., the word was extended to the public domain, to cover not so much the economy of cities and states, but rather their financial management. (See, for example, the beginning of the second book of the *Oeconomica* attributed to Aristotle: Austin and Vidal-Naquet, no. 1B.) The word *oikonomos* could thus be applied not only to the master of an *oikos* but also to whoever was responsible for the treasury or finances of a city or a kingdom. Hesiod, however, had already, in his *Works and Days* (286–319: Austin and Vidal-Naquet, no. 10) written in praise of work. Greeks certainly appreciated effort, expertise, experience, and work well done. They also had words to designate productive action and its products (*ergon* and the verb *ergazesthai*) and also a word for toil or labor (*ponos*). However, they lacked a general term corresponding to our "work" in its abstract sense of a social way of behaving in which all individuals are involved.

The absence of these terms indicates an absence of such concepts. We may find this surprising, given that nowadays we instinctively regard economic activities as cogs in a greater whole, we ascribe dignity to work, and we claim work as a right. But in truth it is our way of seeing things that is exceptional, for it is a relatively recent one. The earliest systematic thinking about the economy appeared in the modern period and eventually led to the science of economics. In the past, among the Greeks in particular, there had been no way of establishing organic links between different economic activities, so these continued to be viewed in all their diversity. The economy was certainly a reality, but it was neither named as a whole nor conceived of as an entity, let alone theorized as a system.

As for "work," the word designated only manual tasks. Those who produced and sold material goods clearly performed a service in society. But they were part of the laboring classes, condemned perforce to such necessities. For the upper strata, the ideal lay elsewhere, in politics, warfare, prayer, or study. Among the Greeks, workers were known as *penētes,* not as "the poor" in the modern sense of the word but rather as "little people" or "humble folk," to use an old-fashioned expression. According to many philosophers, the ideal was *scholē* (from which the word "school" is derived), that is to say, leisure. This was a matter not of idleness, but rather of being spared labor that generated products, leaving one free to devote oneself to tasks of a more elevated nature such as politics (*ta politika,* meaning city affairs), study, or teaching. Wealth, or at any rate a sufficient affluence, constituted an indispensable condition for such a life. Poverty was accordingly a bad thing; wealth, a good one. Yet in truth this ideal created a contradiction.

In cities such as Sparta, the contradiction was resolved by a radical division of functions (Xenophon, *Constitution of the Spartans* 7: Austin and Vidal-Naquet, no. 56). So that citizens could devote themselves to political or military affairs, they were exempted from economic activities, which thus fell to *perioikoi* and Helots. (See below, pp. 40–43). Elsewhere, above all in democratic cities, the greater mass of citizens had to reconcile the obligations of a *homo oeconomicus* (earning a living) and those of a *homo politicus* (being available to take part in warfare and public affairs). According to Thucydides (II.40.2), Pericles, in a speech delivered at the start of the Peloponnesian War, presented that ideal as typically Athenian: "You will find united in the same persons an interest at once in private (*oikeia*) and in public affairs (*politika*), and in others of us who give attention chiefly to business (*erga*), you will find no lack of insight into political matters (*politika*). For we alone regard the man who takes no part in public affairs, not as one who minds his own business, but as good for nothing" (translated by Charles Forster Smith, Loeb Classical Library, 1991). In truth, this ideal was easier to realize in small cities that functioned quite simply than in complex ones such as Athens, where, each year, politics demanded that hundreds of citizens play public parts as members of the council or performing executive duties.

The problem surfaces in the reflections of a number of intellectuals of the classical period. Faithful to the old tradition of Hesiod's *Works and Days,* they presented agriculture as the most noble of productive activities, one that accommodated a way of life worthy of a man of leisure and allowed for the full development of his excellence (*aretē*), in harmony with nature and the divine order (Xenophon, *Oeconomicus* V; Pseudo-Aristotle,

Oeconomica 1343a25–b6). But what they really had in mind was a landowner affluent enough to delegate the daily labors to others. This explains why smaller cultivators were sometimes reckoned to be unworthy of citizenship on account of their life of toil, which deprived them of leisure (e.g., Aristotle, *Politics* 1318b6–21; 1328b41–1329a2 and 1331a32–35). As for the life of craftsmen, those same authors considered it inferior, even demeaning for a citizen, however skillful the craftsman and however beautiful his products. For Xenophon (*Oeconomicus* IV) and Aristotle (*Politics* 1258b35–39 and 1260a39–b2; 1277b1–7 and 1277b33–1278a11; 1328b33–1329a34), for example, the sedentary, laborious, and insalubrious professions of *banausoi* (this term originally meant craftsmen who made use of fire in their work) exerted a pernicious effect on both the body and the soul and created ties of dependency or even servitude with the craftsman's clients, again resulting in a lack of liberty and leisure. Manual labor was not in itself despised, but ideally it had to be undertaken for oneself and not for others (Aristotle, *Politics* 1337b17–23). Finally, commerce, above all the small-scale trading of the *kapēloi* (the agora shopkeepers), aroused the mistrust of many intellectuals. They reproached shopkeepers for their lust for money, their greed for gain, and their dishonesty, and would have liked to limit this profession to foreigners and separate them from citizens so as to distance the citizens from bad influences (e.g., Plato, *Laws* VIII, 847b–d; XI, 918a–919d; and XII, 952d–e; also Aristotle, *Politics* 1327a11–18 and 1331a30–b4). In a famous passage of the *Politics* (1257a41–1258a18), Aristotle reviled the form of trading that he called "chrematistic," perceiving it as a development of the hard reality (*ta ginomena*) of the current situation: for him, this kind of trading was contrary to nature, since the principle and purpose of the exchange was the gaining of money, not the acquisition of goods (as in bartering, where one kind of goods is exchanged for another kind). The whole operation aimed, he thought, solely and unnaturally at profit, the accumulation of limitless sums of money. (Several of the ancient texts mentioned above are reproduced in Austin and Vidal-Naquet, nos. 2, 4, 5, 127, and 128).

Aristotle's view here was clearly moralistic. Similarly, at the beginning of the *Nicomachean Ethics* (I.1, 1094a–b), in which he examines the ultimate aims of existence, Aristotle distinguishes between activities and skills that were admittedly useful but whose purposes were limited, on the one hand, and, on the other, the highest science (*kyriōtatē*), whose particular purposes were manifold and whose overall objective was the common good. The supreme science was politics, to which both medicine, whose purpose was health, and *oikonomia,* whose purpose was wealth, were subordinated. In the *Politics,* Aristotle spelled out the ultimate aim of city life: he called it "living well" (*eu zēn*) or "the perfect and self-sufficient life" (1280b29–1281a2) or "the best possible life," in short "well-being" (*eudaimonia*), which constitutes the perfect realization and use of excellence (*aretē*) (1328a35–b2). In his eyes, the ultimate aim was thus of an ethical nature.

The above judgments were formulated within the Athenian context at a time when the development of craft industries and businesses (see below, p. 138) was provoking reactions in a number of orthodox circles. But the philosophers themselves recognized that attitudes varied from one place to another and that reality was not always in accord with principles (Aristotle, *Politics* 1278a15–26 and 1321a26–31). Indeed, Herodotus (II.167: Austin and Vidal-Naquet, no. 3), while ascribing to the Greeks as a whole a similar disdain for craftsmanlike work as compared to the military profession, had already noted that Sparta openly despised craftsmen, while Corinth disapproved of them the least. In plenty of cities, including Athens itself, many citizens were not landowners and worked either as craftsmen or as traders. Everywhere, the laws governing property decreed that craft workshops had to be owned by citizens. Even notables sometimes dabbled in business. As we shall see, in truth craftsmanlike and commercial activities varied enormously: some provoked scorn, others indifference, yet others respect. In the social hierarchy (see below, p. 38), however, some economic roles (agriculture) tended to be apportioned to citizens, others (craft industries and trade) to foreigners. Even as late as the Roman Empire, land ownership remained the basis of the wealth of "notables."

The Interest of Intellectuals in Economic Matters

In bestowing their approval or disapproval on certain activities, the Athenian intellectuals touched upon economic matters from either an individual or a collective point of view. We know that in the last third of the fifth century B.C. Athens experienced an intellectual upsurge in a number of fields, thanks to the teaching of the Sophists and Socrates, among others. The first economic treatises, *logoi oikonomikoi,* appeared in this context. Xenophon's *Oeconomicus,* which dates from the beginning of the following century but sets Socrates onstage, is the earliest of them to have come down to us. It addresses the management of an *oikos* and, over and above the moral considerations mentioned in the preceding section of this chapter, it also offers technical advice and theoretical reflections. Its technical section (chapters 15 to 19) constitutes a brief treatise on agronomy and belongs to a tradition going back to Hesiod's *Works and Days* that continued to develop after Xenophon (although all the works produced then perished and have unfortunately come down to us only through the Latin agronomists). The theoretical reflections in Xenophon's *Oeconomicus* are interesting, even astonishing, for they diverge from the rigor of other philosophers and reflect more closely the realities of the day. In this treatise, Xenophon presents *oikonomia* right from the start as a branch of knowledge (*epistēmē*) whose purpose is to increase one's wealth, in other words a science of profit. Later, in his *Poroi,* Xenophon proposed measures to rebuild the finances of Athens following its defeat in the War of the Allies (357–355 B.C.) and the loss of its "empire." This treatise shows that the Athenians of the time understood and valued the contributions that metics and the silver mines made to the prosperity of the city and its citizens.

Both Plato and Aristotle repeatedly pondered the use, acquisition, and trading of material goods and the advantages and disadvantages that proximity to the sea presented to a city. Their writings reflect development in their thinking. While continuing to affirm the ideal of the greatest possible self-sufficiency (see Aristotle, *Politics* 1326b26–30), they both recognized that the natural evolution of societies had imposed, as necessities, trading, commerce (both local and distant), and the use of money (Plato, *Republic* II, 370e–371d; *Laws* XI, 918a–c; Aristotle, *Politics* 1327a3–40). At the beginning of the *Politics* (1256a1–1258b8), Aristotle distinguished chrematistics from acquisition that conformed with nature, was part of the *oikonomia,* and was limited to the products necessary for living well (*eu zēn*). Immediately after, however (1258b9–1259a36), in a passage possibly inserted at a later date, he declared that he was moving on from theory to practice and was speaking of the utility of chrematistics in perfectly straightforward terms, rather than returning to his earlier distinction. Finally, in his *Rhetoric* (I.4, 1359b and 1360a), he not only classified provisioning (*trophē*) for the city as one of the five major preoccupations of politicians (along with public resources [*poroi*], war and peace, protection of the territory, and legislation) but also stressed the need for exports (*exagōgē*) and imports (*eisagōgē*) and the usefulness of treaties (*synthēkai*) and conventions (*symbolai*) concluded with other parties. (The point he was making is clear, notwithstanding the ambiguity of certain of his expressions, which are controversial.) Not long before, Xenophon had expressed similar ideas in his *Memorabilia* (III.6.13). The necessity of trade was thus, in a way, integrated into the notion of self-sufficiency, or was at least considered to be inevitably complementary to it.

Those same social circles also manifest an interest in public finances. In his account of the Peloponnesian War, Thucydides frequently stresses the importance of Athens' financial reserves as the foundation of its power (e.g., II.13: Austin and Vidal-Naquet, no. 87). Xenophon in his *Memorabilia* (III.6), Aristotle in his *Rhetoric* (I.4, 1359b), and later one of Aristotle's disciples, in his *Rhetoric to Alexander* (1423a), all claimed that the foremost qualities of a statesman should be a precise understanding of the city's resources and expenditure, together with a concern to balance the two. As for the profound socioeconomic inequalities that more or less constantly divided the citizens as a group (below, pp. 43–46), these also worried philosophers. In the *Politics* (1320a29–b11) and the *Rhetoric to Alexander* (1425b), in particular, Aristotle and one of his disciples drew the attention of statesmen to the need to distribute wealth fairly throughout the city.

The leap from private *oikonomia* to collective aspects of the economy was easily made, given that for most philosophers (with the exception of Aristotle at the beginning of the *Politics* [1252a7–16]) the difference between private and public management was one of mere degree, not of kind. They were happy to draw a parallel between the two, and they stressed the features common to both the *oikonomikos* and the *politikos*. Nevertheless, for Aristotle, as for other philosophers, the economy constituted a secondary domain, primarily private and not meriting the same esteem and attention as politics. Naturally enough, then, they did not judge it necessary to theorize about it; and, in any case, the data needed to do so were not available to them. Their economic thinking was indeed embedded in the context and values of the period.

THE ECONOMIC SPACE OF THE CITIES

Every city (*polis*), sovereign by definition, had its own frontiers, laws, judicial system, taxes, and currency—in short, a whole set of institutions whose essential elements were established in the archaic period, in the course of much legislative activity. A city thus defined the positions and social ranks of all the individuals and groups of which it was composed. It provided the primary framework not only for their rights and obligations, but also for all their activities. The city itself, as a public institution, involved itself in its own economy. The common features of this model are summarized below, along with their principal variants. At the same time, the cities from the start were forced to compromise with their neighbors and with non-Greek peoples and, later, also with other increasingly large and powerful states within which they were progressively incorporated. Although they suffered repercussions from this process, they were not reduced to insignificance. Instead, it created new kinds of balance.

Town and Country

Normally, each city was composed of two complementary entities: the main center of habitation (*asty*), which historians, for convenience' sake, call the urban center even though, in many cases, it was no bigger than a small town or village, and a territory (*chōra*) that supplied at least some of its needs. In principle, every city aspired to be self-sufficient. We shall see below how much that ideal, which at a private level applied equally to every rural plot of cultivated land, was realized in practice.

Many, but not all, settlements were grouped to form towns or villages. Surveys in country areas have revealed not only the presence of isolated farms but also the changes that occurred over the centuries, no doubt as a result of demographic fluctuations and periods of warfare and insecurity. The most striking example is provided by the disappearance of numerous country settlements in European Greece in the late Hellenistic era and under the early Roman Empire, a time when many urban centers were also in decline. (See above, p. 24, and below, p. 84.)

The classic model consisted of a town and its countryside participating interdependently in economic functions. The town would not dominate the rural area, nor was it a parasite upon it. It would therefore be mistaken to characterize the town simply as a consumer, as sometimes happens when the model (*Idealtypus*) proposed by Max Weber and taken over by M.I. Finley is extended in a manner alien to the thinking of the German sociologist. (See below, pp. 63–65). In this respect too, however, there were certainly exceptions to the general rule, in particular in places where dependent peoples cultivated the land for the benefit of the citizens living in the urban center (see the next section of this chapter) or, mutatis mutandis, in the cases of large, highly populated cities that were also royal capitals, such as Alexandria, Antioch, and Pergamum. In accordance with that same model, from the archaic period onward, political and legal equality between the town and the countryside were progressively established. From this point of view, a countryman was the equal of a city dweller, and a small-scale peasant the equal of a large landowner. But that principle was valid only in democracies and where citizens were concerned. And not all the inhabitants of a city were citizens—far from it, for everywhere populations were strictly hierarchical.

The Social Hierarchy

The citizens constituted the heart of the city. Politically speaking, they were not distinct from an abstract State upon which they depended. Rather, they themselves embodied the city every time they gathered in a council or assembly to deliberate and take decisions about public concerns. Furthermore, it was they themselves who were responsible for running the city, since it was they who assumed all executive responsibilities. With some exceptions, they possessed a full set of rights, in particular the right to own land and real estate. They were thus landowners and cultivators in principle. Collectively, they also considered themselves the owners of the city's property and believed that, as such, they had the right to divide it up among themselves. This sense of ownership was in equilibrium, however, with their joint responsibility for the city's debts. The transmission of the title of citizen from father to son required in many cases that the mother also be of citizen stock, which favored endogamy. From the late Hellenistic period onward, the rights to citizenship and real estate were granted more liberally to foreigners, in particular to Romans, and family ties were established between citizens of different cities. By and large, however, over the years the model changed very little.

The rest of the population, in some cases far more numerous, belonged to lower categories and possessed only limited rights. Local situations and statuses varied enormously, and most of their details are unknown to us. In some cities, such as Sparta and the cities of Crete (where archaic structures remained unchanged at least down to the Hellenistic period), citizens might lose some of their civic rights for a variety of reasons and be relegated to lower categories (Thucydides V.34: Austin and Vidal-Naquet, no. 60). In other cities, including Athens, sons born from a citizen father and a foreign mother were classed as foreign residents, whereas in Rhodes and Cos they were regarded as citizens but were denied certain rights.

In general, free wives, even those of citizens, were treated as minors and lived under the guardianship or as a dependent of a man, either a father, a husband, a son, or some other male relative. Their status and freedom of action varied from one city to another. Many women were allowed to acquire and freely possess considerable property. From the Hellenistic period onward, some wealthy women were entrusted with public responsibilities on occasion, or bestowed largesse upon their respective cities. It would be mistaken to see this as a sign of emancipation, however, for public decisions always remained firmly in the hands of the men; women stepped forth from the shadows only as substitutes, to maintain their family's reputation for civic devotion and generosity in the temporary absence of one of those men.

Resident foreigners, known as *metoikoi* (those who live with) in many cities and *paroikoi* (those who live close to) in others, had access to land only as tenants or paid employees. Whether they were Greek or foreign, most of them lived in towns that were open to trading, where they devoted themselves either to craft industries or to commerce, like foreigners just passing through (*xenoi*). In a number of cities, of which Sparta is the best known, communities of *perioikoi* (those living around) were not part of the civic body as such, but were linked to it by various obligations. They were allowed to own land, and they ran their own political affairs. The same went for the *pedieis* (people of the plain) of Priene and the *peroikoi* of Lycia, in southern Asia Minor. During the Hellenistic period, the latter were progressively Hellenized and integrated into the civic body.

At the bottom of the ladder were slaves, denied liberty and regarded as the property of their masters. They made up a large proportion of the labor force in every domain: domestic work, agriculture, craft industries, commerce, public enterprises and services, and so on. Their living conditions varied greatly. Chattel slavery, so called because these men and women were bought and sold in the marketplace, developed more or less everywhere over the centuries, to satisfy the need for a labor force. It also penetrated regions where other forms of servitude prevailed.

These other forms involved not isolated individuals but entire communities that cities had reduced to a state of collective dependence. The status of such groups or peoples, whose details are for the most part unknown to us, varied greatly from one place to another. According to several ancient authors, it hovered somewhere "between liberty and slavery." The communities lived in their own homes on their own land, which they continued to cultivate for their new masters, and they retained certain rights, such as the right of residence and the right to own movable goods. Most of them had also kept a collective name, which in some cases was an ethnic one. In European Greece and the islands, they were found above all in Dorian regions and in central Greece. They included the Helots of Sparta, the Gymnetes of Argos, the Conipodes of Megara, the Penestae of Thessaly, the Mnoïtae and Clarotae of Crete, and so on. The system had originated in distant periods of warfare and conquest. Sometimes it was called into question, for these communities were, after all, Greek. In certain cases, such as that of the Penestae, it evolved: at the end of the fifth century B.C. the Penestae became citizens. In the archaic and Hellenistic periods, similar forms of servitude were imposed upon non-Greek populations by new cities, that is to say, in colonial contexts. These included the Cyllirians of Syracuse, (who were subsequently granted citizenship by the fifth-century tyrants), the Mariandynians of Heraclea Pontica, the Bithynians of Byzantium, the Thracocometae of Cyzicus, the Gergithae of Miletus, the Leleges and Minyans of Tralles, and others. In the East, some similar situations had been inherited from ancient traditions.

The inequality of legal rights may nowadays be found shocking. But in the ancient world it was taken for granted and seldom called into question. Xenophon, in his *Oeconomicus,* reminded his readers that the gods had created men and women as two different, complementary types of creatures: a man was naturally made for outdoor work, a woman for indoor tasks; authority fell to the master of the house, and the woman's role was to organize and oversee all the domestic work. Within this function, and particularly as the mother of a family, a woman would generally be heeded and respected. Slavery and the various forms of servitude did arouse doubts in a number of philosophers, at least where Greek populations were concerned. A natural justification generally prevailed, however, distinguishing Greeks from barbarians and representing the difference between them as an ontological fact: "One that can foresee with his mind is naturally ruler and naturally master, and one that can do these things with his body is subject and naturally a slave" (Aristotle, *Politics* 1252a31–34; transl. by H. Rackham, Loeb Classical Library, 1959). Slaves and dependents had no choice but to accept their lot, which was not inevitably miserable. Although some did rebel and flee their master's house, we know of few organized revolts.

Slavery and servitude were practical necessities, because, ideally, citizens were supposed to liberate themselves from productive work so as to devote themselves to more elevated tasks, in particular to politics. (See above, p. 29.) That is why, as M. I. Finley observed, slavery and the affirmation of citizens' rights developed hand in hand. Should we, on that account, describe this society as "slave-based," as some authors do? That depends on what we mean by the term. It serves well enough to describe a world that depended largely upon slave labor; but it is too strong if it means that the society in question was exclusively or essentially based on this type of labor. Even if slaves and dependents had no social function but to provide an ever-available labor force, the proportion of slaves and dependents varied from one city to another. Moreover and above all, slaves and dependents never did make up the entire labor force: most free men and women had, perforce, to work, and, as we shall see, they frequently did so alongside slaves.

The hierarchy described above reflected a legal and juridical classification, that is to say a scale of "statuses" (to use a term dear to M.I. Finley). The real situation was clearly more complex, for it involved a variety of intersecting distinctions, some derived in particular from unequal distribution of wealth.

Imbalances

Socioeconomic imbalance was a constant factor obtaining in every city. Little is known about the metics' situation, but it clearly varied considerably: although some were wealthy, most belonged to the town's laboring masses. The living conditions of slaves and dependent communities could be deplorable—in the mines, for example, and in certain countrysides in the colonial regions, where great poverty stood in stark contrast to the wealth and well-being of the towns. Everything depended on not only an individual's juridical status, but also his concrete situation, or that of the group to which he belonged. Certain slaves were allocated the most arduous tasks and were often maltreated. Others performed tasks that involved trust, such as the management of the agricultural properties of wealthy citizens (Xenophon, *Oeconomicus* XII) or, in the public domain, caring for the city archives (Aristotle, *The Athenian Constitution* 47.5). Some dependent communities managed to preserve a satisfactory way of life. But all these people were considered inferior and marginal. Their situation stirred no pity and never provoked subversion.

The situation of citizens was quite different, for they could express themselves collectively and lay claim to their rights. In democracies, where citizenship conferred political equality, the imbalance among citizens was linked above all with land ownership. In the archaic period, the disparity was extremely serious, for the best land was at that time monopolized by the rich aristocrats, who also held the political power. The masses, pressured by rapid demographic growth, had to share whatever was left over. Sources refer frequently to the dearth of land, *stenochōria*. Many poor citizens emigrated, seeking land far away. Others fell into debt and then into resulting bondage. Revolts and civil wars drew attention to their complaints, and sometimes debts were written off and land was redistributed. Little by little reforms were introduced to limit the powers of the aristocrats. Although the details of this process elude us, there can be no doubt that land was sometimes confiscated from the rich and distributed among poor citizens. It was in this context that the rights, institutions, laws, and regulations that were to provide the foundations for city life everywhere were first defined, then progressively written down.

Following a period of relative stability, the wars of the classical period reintroduced the very same problems in many regions. Echoes of them are detectable in the last third of the fifth century and above all in the fourth century B.C. Athens, defeated in 404 at the end of the Peloponnesian War, had seen its countryside ravaged by Spartan incursions. Although it never fully recovered the power and wealth of its past, Athens did recover more successfully than other places and once more became the most prosperous city of the age. In Sparta, the crisis was far graver, for, according to Aristotle (*Politics* 1270a16–29), "the land (*chōra*) had passed into a very few hands" as a result of a liberalization of the inheritance laws that had made it possible for two-fifths of a property to pass to women. In this way, numerous citizens lost some of their civic rights (Plutarch, *The Life of Agis* 5: Austin and Vidal-Naquet, no. 106). Elsewhere too, especially in the Peloponnese, we find numerous repercussions of this crisis: unrest, revolts, massacres, exiles, and repeated appeals for the abolition of debts and a redistribution of land, as in the archaic period. Political treaties, in particular the one in 337 between Philip II of Macedon and the cities of the League of Corinth, banned any subversive measures such as confiscation of wealth, redistribution of land, cancellation of debts, or manu-mission of slaves en masse. In default of emigration outlets, some intellectuals recommended the conquest and colonization of the Persian Empire. Many poverty-stricken, uprooted men departed to seek their fortunes as mercenaries. Political exiles became so numerous that in 324, at the Olympic Games, Alexander issued an edict prescribing that all cities recall them. According to Diodorus Siculus (XVIII.8) over 20,000 responded to the summons.

Similar repercussions, accompanied by the same appeals, appeared in the course of the Hellenistic period, particularly in mainland Greece and the islands: they took the form of tensions, revolts, massacres, banishments, tyrannies, appeals to judges summoned from other cities to resolve problems that seemed insurmountable, and so on. In the third century, two kings of Sparta, Agis and Cleomenes, even tried to impose revolutionary measures upon their city. The conflicts of the second half of this period (see above, p. 24) aggravated the situation further. Plutocracies of notables with huge fortunes became established and proceeded to subject the impoverished masses to a sort of economic patronage. Their largesse did provide temporary relief in periods of crisis; but it did nothing to remedy the situation in the long term. Such "euergetism" (benefaction), which was also offered by kings and eventually by emperors, became increasingly common up to the time of the Roman Empire, peaking in the second century A.D. Despite the generosity of emperors and elite groups now Romanized, however, the problem never was resolved. Inequalities, underemployment, poverty, and indebtedness all persisted, and the wealthy continued to be haunted by fear of disorders.

These conflicts have sometimes been analyzed as class struggles, in the Marxist sense. In truth, though, this type of explanation does not suit the Greek world, whose economy was quite unlike modern capitalism. This question, however, is much debated and cannot be tackled here.

Private, Public, and Sacred Space

The Greeks regularly distinguished between what belonged to a private individual, *idios,* and what was common to all, *koinos.* In many economic and financial texts, they often used the term *dēmosios* to designate whatever belonged to the *dēmos* or "the citizen people," regarded as a political entity. For example, city funds were known as the *dēmosia chrēmata.* Those distinctions correspond well enough to our own categories of what is "private" and what is "public," if one takes into account the fact, emphasized above (pp. 38–39), that the group of citizens as a whole corresponded to what we call "the state." But the Greeks further distinguished that which belonged to the gods or was consecrated to them and was known as *hieros*. The expression *hiera chrēmata* can thus be translated as "sacred funds." When applied to the city as a whole, the three adjectives *idios, koinos,* and *hieros* designated three categories of goods and spaces, categories that remained unchanged right down the ages and were to be found, to varying degrees, in every city. The distinction is clearly made, for example, in Aristotle's *Politics* (1267b33–37), where he describes the division of the territory made by Hippodamus of Miletus. Most economic activities were left to the private sector, although interactions between the private, the public, and the sacred abounded.

The private space, which was generally the most extensive, was naturally at the disposal of the private individuals who inhabited it and exploited it. As we have noted, with very few exceptions, only citizens could become landowners here. Sacred space comprised real estate in the form of both land and buildings (temples and sanctuaries, land used for agriculture and pasturage, farms, and houses) and also movable goods (valuable reserves consisting of a variety of objects and, as time passed, money, accumulated through donations from both cities and private individuals, many of them consisting of first fruits from the harvest or shares of booty). Every item (or group of items) belonged to a particular deity. In reality, the goods were administered by the community that used the sanctuary (such as a deme, for example), one or more families, or, in some cases, a whole group of cities, as at Delphi. Sacred land was normally marked out by boundary posts, *horoi,* in the same way as city land.

As for public space, this belonged specifically to the city. In addition to real estate, it comprised equipment and buildings refurbished or constructed out of public funds: ports, wharves, warehouses, shipyards, ships, arsenals, marketplaces, streets, roads, porticoes, fountains, cisterns, theaters, gymnasia, fortifications, mines, quarries, and so on. All these amenities were obviously for common use, and many of them provided what we may call infrastructures for the cities' economic activities. In just the same way as the sacred land, farms, and houses, many of these amenities were administered by private individuals to whom they were rented out or conceded. They included land, farms, houses, porticoes (or, to be more precise, their workshops and shops), mines, and quarries. For sanctuaries and cities alike, such amenities represented sources (*poroi*) of revenue (*prosodoi*), both in kind and in money.

As for the sanctuaries' reserves of precious objects and revenues, they were normally used to finance cults; in many cases a proportion of them was carefully hoarded. Some particularly wealthy sanctuaries, such as those of Athens and Delos, could provide credit by lending money through the intermediary of the public administration, either to inhabitants of the city, or to the city itself, or to other cities. (See below, p. 127.) In sanctuaries as in cities, a relatively large work force, mostly composed of slaves—both public and sacred—was employed in the upkeep of places (buildings, streets, porticoes), the running of cults (daily manual tasks), and administrative routine (keeping archives, collecting taxes, and so on). Cities would, moreover, often undertake public projects, such as the erection of certain buildings. (See below, p. 107.) Through their many activities, and their provision of loans backed by assets of both real estate and movable goods, sanctuaries and cities thus engendered numerous economic activities, even if they were not themselves directly productive.

Taxation and Public Expenditure

The primary source (*poros*) of revenue (*prosodoi*) for cities, however, was taxation, which targeted economic activities above all. The ancient origin of taxation went back to the contributions in kind that community leaders, in the Mycenaean and subsequent periods, levied on the possessions or products of private individuals. Little by little, taxation became a feature of the public domain (*koinon*), acquiring its more or less definitive form in the archaic period, a time when public institutions were taking shape and the use of minted money was spreading. From that point on, for centuries, the city was the basic milieu for taxation. Documents from the classical period suggest that taxes were already very diversified and were divided unequally among the various categories of the population. One view still largely accepted today holds that citizens considered regular payment of direct taxes to be degrading. Certainly, the tax on wealth (*eisphora*) to which they were subjected in some cities was exceptional and was not imposed regularly. The wealthiest citizens were encouraged to contribute generous benefactions when they assumed the executive responsibilities and "liturgies" entrusted to them (public services such as the equipping and manning of warships, the organization of choruses and festivals, and so on), adding their own personal contributions to the funds placed at their disposal. (See, for example, Xenophon, *Oeconomicus* II.5–8: Austin and Vidal-Naquet, no. 97.) But in fact, more often than is generally acknowledged, citizens were also subjected to taxes imposed either on their assets (land, houses, slaves, flocks, draft animals, apiaries, etc.) or on their products (grain, wine, oil, milk, fruits, vegetables, wood, fodder, etc.). True enough, some cities received sufficient revenues from their mines (Thasos, for example) or from the taxes they imposed on trading (Athens) to be able to abolish or reduce that kind of taxation. In other trading cities, however, such as Miletus, Teos, and Telmessus, citizens did have to pay direct taxes. Dependent communities (see above, p. 41) were naturally subjected to the same obligations, often providing payment in kind.

Even so, indirect taxation was the more widespread; one comes across varying degrees of it everywhere. Its organization and structure changed little over the centuries. It hit commercial transactions above all, and this affected the entire population, since taxes were reflected in retail prices. In the first place, all imported or exported merchandise was subject to customs dues, usually at the rate of 2 percent (one-fiftieth, the *pentēkostē*). The managers (*epimelētai*) of a market (*emporion*) received statements (*apographai*) from the traders and, following evaluation of the merchandise, the collectors of the one-fiftieth tax (*pentēkostologoi*), usually private individuals to whom this responsibility was farmed out, undertook to collect it. The yield from the tax naturally varied from one city to another and from one year to another, depending on the volume of trade. Our sources have preserved a number of relevant figures. In Athens, around 400 B.C., in the aftermath of the Peloponnesian War, when activity in Piraeus had slumped, the farmed-out *pentēkostē* brought in 36 talents (Andocides, *On the Mysteries* 133–34: Austin and Vidal-Naquet, no. 91). Taking into account the tax farmers' cut, this means that foreign trade that year was estimated at over 1,500 talents or 9 million drachmas. (The talent was a sum, or rather a weight, of silver, which was worth 6,000 drachmas in the Attic system.) The *pentēkostē* of Delos, a much smaller city, brought in no more than 14,200 drachmas in 279 B.C. and 17,900 the following year. But other taxes, at similar rates, were also levied on the use of port facilities, such as anchorage and towing, or simply as dues for passing through the port (*diagōgia* or *paragōgia*). These are known from Byzantium (in some periods, at least) and from Corinth (for haulage over the *Diolkos,* from one port to another). Port charges are mentioned in numerous texts, for in many cities they played an important role. According to Polybius (XXX.31.12), before the creation of the free port of Delos in 166, the charges levied by Rhodes used to bring in 1 million drachmas.

Retail trade was taxed at the point where retailers (*kapēloi*) were buying from wholesale merchants (*emporoi*) products that they would then sell on in the agora. There were *epōnia* or taxes on transactions (sales, renting, farming out, etc.), dues on spaces for stalls, charges for using certain kinds of public equipment, such as official weighing machines, etc.). There were a great many of these taxes, but the burden obviously varied from one city to another. To them should be added tolls charged for entering and leaving by the city gates (*diapylia*), personal or poll taxes, some of which affected citizens, metics (*metoikion*), and craftsmen. But we know few specifics about them, apart from the Athenian *metoikion,* which amounted to one drachma per month for men and half a drachma for women.

The expenses of cities and sanctuaries were numerous and heavy: they had to pay for public and sacred slaves, remunerate citizens who took on certain political responsibilities, finance the troops, award prizes for the winners of competitions, purchase animals for sacrifices as well as various items used in religious cults, construction materials for public buildings and ships, grain and oil to sell on or distribute, and so on. As both an employer and an entrepreneur, a city would play a major role in promoting the circulation of goods and money. Distribution of its expenditure was naturally adapted to current needs and circumstances. Thus, public purchases of grain and oil increased in the Hellenistic period (see below, p. 167), while military expenses were generally covered by the kingdoms. With the advent of the *pax Romana,* these obviously diminished. As we shall see below (pp. 60–62), the effects of foreign domination had a particular impact in this domain.

The economic and financial roles played by cities could thus be very diverse. The Primitivist school of thought has often stressed the incoherence and neglect that appear to have prevailed in public finances, placing cities in permanently straitened positions. It is true that Greek management differed considerably from ours nowadays, and that it was frequently improvisatory. The second book of the *Oeconomica* attributed to Aristotle registers an astonishing abundance of expedients of every kind, mostly confiscations, manipulations, and extortions. (Austin and Vidal-Naquet, no. 91, provide several examples.) A number of inscriptions also record instances of embezzlement and negligence. By the end of the Hellenistic period, many cities had seen their finances ruined by warfare and payment of ensuing indemnities. The corruption of certain magistrates was such that Roman governors were forced to intervene. Later on, emperors had to take steps to remedy waste and faulty management by sending in *curatores* and *correctores* or even by placing a city under their direct guardianship.

The sources tend to describe exceptions and difficulties more frequently than routine circumstances. At the same time, however, they often record efforts that citizens themselves made to reestablish order and balance in public finances and even the general prosperity of their respective cities. In the fourth century, for example, the Athenians gradually modernized their management methods, making them more centralized. Whereas, around 350, in the wake of the War between the Allies, public revenues had fallen to 130 talents, by ten years later they had risen to the earlier level of 400 talents (Demosthenes, *Fourth Philippic* 37–38), doubtless thanks to the administration of Eubulus. Lycurgus, put in charge of finances from 338 to 326, increased them to 1,200 or possibly even 1,575 talents (Pseudo-Plutarch, *The Lives of the Ten Orators* 842F and 852B). Hellenistic inscriptions record similar efforts, for instance attempts to end the abuses of certain tax farmers (in Colophon, in the first half of the third century) or to correct falsified archives (in Paros, late third century). Moreover, as we have seen, quite a few cities and sanctuaries proved capable of accumulating reserves and surpluses. In emergencies, all the cities could resort to such methods as imposition of exceptional taxes, borrowing, calling for contributions, and, mainly in later periods, appealing to the beneficence of prominent citizens, kings, or emperors. Such tactics, many of which appealed to the loyalty and generosity of private individuals, lent the system a measure of flexibility. Furthermore, many texts mention the procedure of sharing out (*diataxis* or *merismos*) which estimated future expenses every year and kept a watchful eye on the good management of finances.

In normal times, not only were the cities concerned to balance their expenses and their incomes, but in general they managed to do it just as well as we do.

The fact remains, nevertheless, that the taxation system was inflexible. Citizens knew how to spread the load of taxation such as the tax on real estate, liturgies, and the *eisphora,* adjusting them in proportion to the individuals' wealth. They were likewise capable of adapting or reforming their administrative methods. It never occurred to them, though, to modify the system itself or to modulate it in a selective fashion, for example by lowering or abolishing certain taxes to protect or benefit certain types of products or to favor exports and imports. The best example here is provided by the *pentēkostē,* which always applied equally to whatever goods came into the city and whatever left it. This constituted an obstacle to the importation of crucial supplies. The only real innovation, in the Hellenistic and imperial periods, was the ever-increasing role played by euergetism in exceptional circumstances. But citizens never desisted from farming out the collection of most taxes, usually for one year, to tax farmers (*telōnai*). These individuals, many of whom had already become wealthy by other means, naturally treated this business as a source of personal enrichment. They would send their slaves out to cover the particular terrain allotted to them and were not necessarily averse to abusive methods of collection. It would be anachronistic to deplore such stagnation or to criticize the Greeks for never having thought of using taxation for social ends, for instance by introducing a fairer distribution of the wealth in private hands. The system was suited to the mindset of the time and to a purely fiscal view of taxation, according to which its purpose was simply to fund public needs.

Money: Minting and Legislation

The minting of coins invited public intervention and legislative control of mints. We shall see (pp. 120–22) how the use of money came to spread in trading, but first let us consider its origins. The period in which minted coins were first produced is a matter of controversy, but it is now agreed by most scholars to have been quite late, at the end of the seventh century B.C. or perhaps the beginning of the sixth. According to Herodotus (I.94), minting money was not a Greek idea but came from the Lydians, a people of western Asia Minor whose capital was Sardis and whose last king was the famous Croesus. Ionian cities such as Ephesus, Miletus, and Teos were soon imitating the Lydian kings, and it is here that the earliest coins were found. They were made of electrum, a natural or artificial alloy of gold and silver. The earliest coins of pure gold or silver appeared around the mid-sixth century and are traditionally attributed to King Croesus and known as creseides; but some of these may have been issued by the king of Persia, Cyrus the Elder, or even by Darius, his successor. After 550, a number of Greek cities followed this example, first Aegina, Athens, and Corinth—all maritime trading cities—and then others in southern Italy and Sicily. Between 520 and 480, the use of coins spread widely and rapidly and became increasingly the rule even in cities as distant as Cyrene and Marseilles as well as among non-Greek peoples in Asia Minor and Thrace. Some cities, Sparta for one, were slow to welcome coinage, but the Greek world in general increasingly adopted it as a regular tool. Following an important phase of internal development and expansion in the Mediterranean region, many cities were by this time sufficiently mature to do this, for they had built the kind of political, juridical, economic, and fiscal framework necessary for the diffusion of money. For example, according to Herodotus, who contrasted this to the situation of communities in the Persian kingdom (I.153), the presence of a central agora in which trading took place was characteristic of Greek cities.

The invention of minting has been the subject of much controversy. Traditionally, two explanations for it are put forward, one commercial, the other political. There is an obvious tendency to believe that commerce was the domain in which the use of minted money was most likely spontaneous. This was certainly the view of Herodotus (I.94), who went on to add (wrongly, but never mind at this point) that the Lydians were the first retail traders (*kapēloi*). In the following century, Aristotle took a similar view in his *Politics* (1257a31–b5). Minted money certainly did introduce more flexibility and convenience: coins, which were calibrated uniformly and had a value that depended on their weight and imprint and was guaranteed by an official stamp, constituted an instrument whose worth was indisputable and not hard to calculate, and that could be easily carried about and exchanged. It is not clear, however, that money had a commercial vocation right from the start. In his *Nicomachean Ethics* (1132b21–1133b28: Austin and Vidal-Naquet, no. 44), Aristotle related its adoption to a question of social justice and explained it by the need to evaluate such exchanges of services as were a feature of social life. Now, it is true that the earliest coins minted were of high value: they were staters (each worth two drachmas) or tetradrachmas (four drachmas). This is why many studies have, reasonably enough, stressed the political dimension of the payments made with these coins: the pay of mercenaries, the wages of workers, the purchase of materials for public constructions, the distribution of surpluses to citizens, the collection of taxes, fines, rents, debt repayments, and various other charges. In a wider sense, the development of democracies, and hence of civic order and justice, no doubt favored the diffusion of this new tool, while the tool itself encouraged the establishment of certain institutions. Recent research, however, has surprisingly revealed that small silver coins were minted in Asia Minor as early as the second half of the sixth century, and in far greater quantities than had previously been expected. We also know that small silver coins appeared in European Greece in the following century, as did the earliest bronze coins, which were of low value and date from the end of the fifth century. So minted money was used in small local transactions at a very early date.

But the commercial explanation has its limits. After all, trading did not wait for minted money to appear before it developed, using nonmonetary methods of evaluation; it had been going on for a long time already. For close to two thousand years, the Mesopotamian world, which had reached a high level of evolution, had been using weighty standards in the form of ingots and bars or lumps of silver. It managed perfectly well with this anonymous money, which bore no markings, carried no official guarantees, and required extremely precise weighing and checking. And for centuries, the Greeks themselves, who were in contact with the Near East, had been evaluating things (and women, according to Hesiod and Homer) in terms not only of, for example, heads of cattle, but also by means of a variety of precious objects: cauldrons, tripods, double-headed axes, weighed ingots of gold, silver, or electrum, and so forth. One such object was an iron spit or *obelos,* whose name subsequently came to designate an obol, one-sixth of a drachma. (The latter word also meant a "fistful" or a "jugful.") Indeed, one whole century before the creation of minted money, the Greeks were using weighed pieces of silver as standards. All these means of evaluation already constituted "money" in the wider sense. So even if coinage introduced a new commodity, it did not have the revolutionary impact that is often attributed to it.

G. Le Rider recently has convincingly developed a theory that he had presented earlier: namely that a state issuing minted coins would be able to make a profit. Putting the coins into circulation, the city would set a nominal (arbitrary) value on them, one that was higher than their intrinsic worth (which corresponded with their actual weight). In Athens, for example, the discrepancy was in excess of 5 percent in the fifth century. The profit thus realized took into account the cost of manufacture and included a tax that was the equivalent of what subsequent ages were to call "seigneuriage." It is clear that cities also sometimes minted coins that were slightly lighter than their canonical weight. The value of these was thus partly a matter of trust, and they could not be used outside their city of origin. Furthermore, a city would often impose the use of its own currency within its territory. Foreign visitors were thus obliged to change their money, and the city levied a tax upon such transactions. The expectation of such profits, which is clearly reflected in texts of a later date, played a decisive role. That is why, right from the start, cities made the minting of money a public privilege. To stamp coins with the city's emblem was therefore a state act and was always the responsibility of a magistrate. It affirmed the city's identity and pride. The profitability of minting money was thus complemented by a political dimension—a point that G. Le Rider also emphasizes. That dimension continued to play its part, mutatis mutandis, even when a city was incorporated into a vaster state that minted its own money. (See below, pp. 122 and 125.) Cities usually decided to mint coins with a view to their own expenses, but occasionally they did so simply to mark some important festival or anniversary.

Given this context, it is logical to suppose that minting took place in public workshops. However, we know very little about these. The Athens mint is mentioned, in several texts, always in the singular, *argyrokopeion*. It was certainly public property, as is shown both by a fifth-century decree imposing the Athenian currency upon the allies of the League of Delos (see below, pp. 123–24) and by a fragment of Andocides (no. 5, scholium to Aristophanes' *Wasps* 1007), which notes that a public slave (*dēmosios*) worked there. The mint was located in the agora and also housed the official city weights. The currency decree also alludes (again in the singular) to the respective mints of each of the allied cities. Although the term *argyrion* refers to silver, the same equipment was used for minting gold and bronze, for *argyrion* designated not only silver but also money in general (just as does the French term *argent*). Traces of such mints have been found on the fringes of agoras at Argos and Pella. The kings of Macedon, the Hellenistic kingdoms, and later the Roman emperors all had their own mints, but many royal and imperial currencies were minted in the cities as well. It also seems that mobile workshops would follow armies and emperors on the move. (The equipment was quite lightweight.) As issues of coins were intermittent, smaller cities would sometimes entrust the work, and their own stamps, to larger ones. Since private workshops known as *argyrokopeia* or *chrysochoieia* also existed, working on gold and silver destined for a variety of uses (precious tableware, jewelry, etc.), it is possible that, where necessary, some cities may have entrusted the minting of their respective currencies to these private workshops, to be effected according to their official directives and under official supervision.

Cities thus provided money with a legal framework, regulating its creation and usage. Not all cities needed to mint their own money, but each could legislate in this domain and, indeed, did so frequently, with a view to legitimating currencies in their own territories by declaring them to be *dokimon* (reliable) or, conversely, rejecting them as *adokimon* (unreliable). In 375/4, following both a decrease in the issue of coins since its defeat in 404 and also an influx of imitations and counterfeit coins, Athens passed a law defining the conditions of validity for silver coins with the Athenian stamp. Cities would also regulate the modalities for exchanging one currency against another and, in some cases, would fix the rate of exchange and prescribe places where such transactions should take place (for example, Olbia: Austin and Vidal-Naquet, no. 103). Some cities (Byzantium and Chalcedon, for example) even managed to monopolize money-changing operations, thereby creating a new source of revenue for themselves.

The Expansion of Economic Spheres

As the centuries passed, many cities became accustomed to foreign domination or to domination by powers grouped into alliances and federations. In all such cases, they agreed more or less freely to forgo some of their own powers and to contribute to common expenses. Such situations relate primarily to political history, and they pose an often-debated problem that is not too be tackled as a whole in the present work, the problem of the liberty and autonomy of allied or dependent cities. But those situations were also strongly reflected in the fiscal sphere. For instance, the cities that became Athens' allies in the classical period paid Athens financial contributions that were earmarked for their common defense. Between 188 and 167 B.C., Rhodes derived large revenues from the regions of Caria and Lycia, which it had been given by Rome. The cities absorbed by Hellenistic kingdoms received varied treatment from their kings depending on whether they were ancient or new, and whether they were considered to be free or subject states: usually subject states had to pay the kingdoms an overall contribution in the form of tribute (*phoros*) or a specified proportion of their taxes, or both. Similarly, under the Roman Empire, certain cities were free and exempt or partly exempt from taxes, whereas others were subject to both a *tributum soli* (real-estate tax) and *tributum capitis* (poll tax). In particular designated places in each province or administrative region, indirect taxes were also levied, above all the *portoria* or customs dues, many of which took over from taxes formerly levied by the kings.

As a result of all this, considerable funds and wealth were transferred to the central power. The scale of these transfers is impossible to evaluate, for no data are available beyond exceptional cases like fifth-century Athens. But we know for certain that the impact varied greatly. In the classical and Hellenistic periods, some cities complained of being burdened by the *phoros*. In Caria and Lycia, revolts broke out against Rhodes. In the late Hellenistic period, many cities suffered from the harsh exactions of tax collectors. (See above, p. 24). But some cities were treated with deference and fairness, and the advent of the Roman Empire put an end to excesses. Besides, in exchange, most cities benefited from the military protection that their respective masters provided. In times of need, particularly after a disaster such as an earthquake or when food was in short supply, they could count on aid from the kings and emperors. Even in normal times, subject cities regularly received aid from a number of Hellenistic sovereigns. Furthermore, a proportion of the sums levied was, in many cases, spent on the spot or in the surrounding region, mainly for the upkeep of troops, oil supplies for the gymnasia, and urban development. All this helped to lighten city expenses, and, as the sums levied were returned into circulation, they stimulated city production and trade. These effects are particularly evident under the empire, when, thanks to the *pax Romana,* imperial taxation may have played a positive role and increased production. But the most important point to note is that, in all these situations, even dependent cities were able to preserve part of their autonomy and, along with their local responsibilities and expenses, at least a margin of initiative. Within their own frontiers, they remained fiscal entities that for the most part themselves collected all local taxes, by the traditional system of tax farming; they then divided the income between the sums due to their respective masters and those over which they retained full control. This situation persisted even as late as the empire, despite all Rome's interventions and the controls that it imposed in the domain of local finances.

Those federations and foreign domination entailed even wider consequences for production and trade. In the classical period, Athens certainly had no ambition to dominate the

Aegean world other than politically. But from that political dominance it derived great economic and financial power, and its port became the busiest in the eastern Mediterranean. (See below, p. 132.) New trading networks were established and the Aegean cities had perforce to adapt to them. The impact upon their local activities was probably limited, however. A similar situation obtained for Rhodes, whose economy dominated the Aegean world in the early Hellenistic period. Structural changes and new balances were the result of several factors. These included the heavy influence, first, of the Hellenistic kingdoms and capitals, then of Rome, which soon became the sole capital city. Other factors included the scale of production, commerce, and consumption, the redistribution of trading networks, the euergetism of kings and emperors, the foundation of Roman colonies, and the prosperity or decline of certain cities. The impact of all this certainly varied from one region to another. It was felt above all in the spheres of agriculture and trade (see below, pp. 132–33) and was particularly painful in European Greece, which experienced a veritable slump lasting until the advent of the empire. But production and trade still depended, to a large extent, upon a vast network of active cities whose role and importance were never brought into question by the kings and emperors.

Citizens' Interventions in the Economy

We have now seen how great a role the cities played over more than a millennium, even in a world that was rapidly expanding. Not only did the cities remain the framework for numerous economic activities, but they also preserved a large measure of initiative: in the management of their public and sacred spheres, in taxation on produce and trading, and, at least to some degree, on the minting of money and monetary legislation. In the chapters that follow, we shall be examining the role that cities played in agriculture, in public enterprises, and above all in commerce. Citizens were very conscious of the impact of the decisions they took in all these domains. But the fundamental question concerns their motives. On this subject, scholars are virtually unanimous. Citizens did entertain preoccupations of an economic nature, but in general these were intermingled with or subordinated to wider political or social objectives. Furthermore, their preoccupations corresponded above all to current needs and circumstances. There was no unified attitude based on any overall views of the problems and of what was at stake, nothing that could be described as an economic policy. They certainly did not aim for generalized growth in the economy, for the Greeks had not theorized such activities into a system and did not perceive how the various elements interacted. The preoccupations of Greek citizens reflect no economic agenda of any kind, not even one of laissez-faire. There was nevertheless a logic behind them, and they all had one priority in common: the interests of the citizens themselves. For it was the citizens who monopolized both power and responsibility for the city's collective institutions. The other inhabitants, in particular the metics, who did after all play an important economic role, had no means to act as a group, so could exert pressure only as individuals or families. Possibly the corporations to which they belonged might also act as pressure groups, but we possess no evidence to document this. Economic decisions taken in council or in assembly thus reflected above all the immediate preoccupations of the citizens. In this respect, the

Poroi is most revealing: when Xenophon proposed that the Athenians should facilitate commercial activities and intensify the exploitation of the Laurion mines (Austin and Vidal-Naquet, no. 96), his aim was simply to increase public revenues. It is in this sense, rather than any wider one (see above, p. 38), that the Weberian model of a consumer city seems relevant.

PRIMARY TEXT
The City and Its Territory

As to the question of what particular kind of land [a city] ought to have, it is clear that everybody would commend that which is most self-sufficing (and such is necessarily land that bears every sort of produce, for self-sufficiency means having a supply of everything and lacking nothing). In extent and magnitude the land ought to be of a size that will enable the inhabitants to live a life of liberal and at the same time temperate leisure. . . . The proper configuration of the country is not difficult to state (though there are some points on which the advice of military experts also must be taken): on the one hand it should be difficult for enemies to invade and easy for the people themselves to march out from. And in addition, on the other hand, the same thing holds good for the territory that we said about the size of the population: it must be well able to be taken in at one view, and that means being a country easy for military defense. As to the site of the city, if it is to be ideally placed, it is proper for it to be well situated with regard both to the sea and to the country. One defining principle is that mentioned above: the city must be in communication with all parts of the territory for the purpose of sending out military assistance; and the remaining principle is that it must be easily accessible for the conveyance to it of the agricultural produce and also of timber-wood and any other such material that the country happens to possess.

As for communication with the sea, it is in fact much debated whether it is advantageous to well-ordered states or harmful. It is maintained that the visits of persons brought up under other institutions are detrimental to law and order, and so also is a swollen population, which grows out of sending out abroad and receiving in a number of traders, but is unfavorable to good government. Now, it is not difficult to see that, if these consequences are avoided, it is advantageous, in respect of both security and the supply of necessary commodities, that the city and the country should have access to the sea.

Aristotle, *Politics* 1326b27–1327a20, translated by
H. Rackham, The Loeb Classical Library, 1959

TWO

The World of Agriculture

Throughout antiquity, agriculture remained the basis of city economies. As in all barely mechanized rural societies, Greek agriculture required a large workforce, especially at harvesting and grape-picking times, and it occupied a large majority of the population, probably at least 80 percent. Agriculture provided a high proportion of the raw materials for craftsmen and for commerce. It shaped landscapes, marked societies, and pervaded customs and *mores*. Throughout history, it remained par excellence the domain of citizens' activity, for it was they who, collectively and publicly, possessed the land, always considering land ownership to be their more or less exclusive right. On many occasions, they even took political decisions designed to provide land for citizens who lacked it. This was effected either by dividing up existing plots or else by founding colonies or cleruchies (allotting plots of land [*klēroi*] situated outside the city). Throughout history, land ownership had always constituted the basis of most large fortunes.

More than any other economic activity, work on the land was stamped with ethical values (see above, p. 30), conservatism, and routine. It followed the unchanging rhythm of the seasons, festivals, and rituals. Permanent fear of drought and diseases affecting crops and herds encouraged agricultural workers to stick to well-tried approaches rather than take any risks. Virtually everywhere, natural conditions (see above, pp. 15–18) imposed the constraints of intensive dry agriculture, whose yields could be increased only by maximizing exploitation of the arable land and increasing the labor force.

Yet, though there were common features, the world of agriculture was neither uniform nor static. Soils and rainfall varied from one region to another, necessitating adaptations and choices. Types of agriculture and agricultural properties varied and, over the years, they evolved. Up until the third century B.C., pressures of demography and urbanization led cities to enlarge the area of agricultural land. As we have seen above (pp. 18–20), techniques for processing agricultural produce did make some progress. From the classical period onward, methods of cultivation also improved: witness the appearance of agronomy, botany, and diet manuals, and the Greeks who experimented with adapting new species to production in the Egyptian Faiyum during the third century B.C.

AGRICULTURAL LABOR AND PRODUCTS
The Crops

Over the centuries, the classic Mediterranean triad of crops (cereals, vines, and olive trees) had become well established. That triad always did preponderate, but the Greeks grew other types of produce too, leguminous plants in particular. Agricultural tasks demanded constant attention throughout the year. Their rhythm was dictated by the Mediterranean climate.

The cultivation of cereals went back to the Neolithic period. The two dominant varieties were wheat (*pyros*) and barley (*krithai*). The Greeks lumped them together, using the general term *sitos* (which is therefore better translated as "grain" or "cereals," rather than "wheat"). A type of soft wheat, the equivalent of our top-quality wheat, did exist, but hard wheat was more common. Wheat required better soil and greater humidity than barley, whose deeper roots helped it ripen more rapidly and yield better harvests. The most widely cultivated variety corresponded to today's winter barley. After the grain harvests (April–June), land was generally left to lie fallow for over a year. In the spring, when the rains diminished, the land was prepared by early plowing: a plow (or a hoe) dug into the soil, tearing up and burying stubble and weeds, which served as a green fertilizer. More plowing, with a similar purpose and to enrich the soil, was undertaken during the summer. The first autumn rains signaled the sowing of seed, following a preliminary plowing that opened up furrows and a second that covered the seeds with earth. (The harrow did not appear until later.) The rains of winter promoted germination, and the plants were weeded. Harvesting took place at the start of the dry season, barley in April and May (at least in warmer regions) and wheat in May and June. After the harvest came flailing, winnowing, and storage of the grain. Along with barley and wheat, two varieties of millet were frequently cultivated. Millet was sown in the spring and ripened during the summer. A number of attempts have been made to estimate the yield of cereal cultivation on the basis of the few figures we possess for Attica, but the hypotheses constructed in this way are fragile and contradictory, so let us ignore them.

Vine cultivation, introduced later, dated back to the Bronze Age. The vine could adapt to dry, stony soils but required a great deal of work and attention. The grape harvest began in September and October. Hesiod (*Works and Days* 609–14) recommended exposing the bunches of grapes to the sun for ten days, then keeping them in the shade for five more, to produce a dry liqueur wine. Crushing the grapes, then making and storing the wine and the products made from the marc and lees took months; the work often went on well into the winter or even the spring, when cuttings were pruned and spaced out, followed by plowing and fertilizing the soil.

Olive trees did not really begin to spread until the archaic period. Like vines, they thrived on thin soil. But they took twenty or so years to grow to maturity and even then produced fruit only one year in two. The area for olive trees was relatively limited, for they could not thrive in temperatures lower than 3° C (37.4°F) or in violent winds like the summer *meltemi* that blew from north of the Aegean Sea. The earliest harvesting of green olives began in September and October. Harvesting ripe olives began in November and continued into the winter months, as did the crushing and pressing of the olives. In winter moments unoccupied by other tasks, there was pruning to be done, and the soil would be hoed and fertilized. Old olive trees were cut right back to the stump to encourage new shoots.

Vegetables and leguminous plants left fewer traces and have captured the interest of researchers only recently, but they were more important than used to be believed. They were of many different kinds: onions, celery, cabbages, cucumbers, leeks, turnips, fennel, horseradishes, peas, beans, broad beans, vetch, lentils, garlic, and aromatic herbs (bay, sage, savory, mint, thyme, marjoram, rosemary, coriander, and basil, etc., which all grew wild). Green vegetables had to be consumed swiftly and were probably cultivated in gardens, where they could be watered. Other plants, such as flax, sesame, and poppies, were cultivated either for their seeds or for their oil. Some vegetables and leguminous plants ripened in the winter. Others, such as turnips, broad beans, chickpeas, lentils, vetch, horseradish, flax, sesame, and millet, all sown from April onwards, would ripen in the course of the summer.

The cultivation of plants used as fodder depended on the scale of local stock-raising (see next section): grass (for hay), lupins, laburnum (which bore nourishing leaves), alfalfa (which seems to have been brought from Persia in the fifth century B.C. and was not widely grown), leguminous plants such as vetch, cereals such as *zeia,* a type of spelt that was fed to horses . . . In addition, most farms probably cultivated fruit trees, which also require time-consuming care. Fruits and nuts ripened during the summer: apples, pears, cherries, plums, blackberries, melons, hazelnuts, pistachio nuts, chestnuts, and so on. Plants used by craftsmen were also cultivated or gathered: flax, willows, rushes, reeds, and several species used for dyeing. Many of these were found and gathered in the forests or on scrubland and marshland by women and children in their free moments.

The Greeks had few means of fertilizing the soil. Animal dung was available only when beasts were kept in stables or were pastured on land lying fallow. In default of such manure, quicklime, saltpeter, or scraps of leather might be used. More frequently, farmers burned weeds and turned straw and grasses under to serve as green fertilizer. Compost of a kind was made out of the plants that grew on land left fallow and the bushes found on stony wasteland. So as not to exhaust the earth used for cultivation, land would be left fallow, generally every two years, which allowed the soil to rest for sixteen months. Such land could also be sown with fodder plants that were then plowed in as green fertilizer. More rarely, leguminous plants or the seeds of summer fodder plants would be sown on out-of-the-way land set aside for cultivation. Apart from all this, if the gaps left between rows of vines or olive trees were wide enough, growers cultivated cereals or leguminous plants there. Agricultural practices thus varied widely.

Stock-raising

In his *Oeconomicus* (V.3), Xenophon states that stock-raising is linked to agriculture. The expression he uses, *probateutikē technē,* mainly means raising sheep and goats (*probata*). Numerous texts, both literary and epigraphical, mention not only those two species but also pigs, poultry (chickens and geese), cows, oxen, donkeys, and mules (the last three being draft animals or beasts of burden), and also horses (luxury mounts, and horses used for hunting and warfare). The domestication of such creatures was as ancient as agriculture. Smaller animals, better adapted by inclusive diets to the Mediterranean vegetation, were far more numerous than the larger ones, as they are today. It is not easy to estimate the importance of stock-raising in comparison to agriculture or to see exactly how the two were linked. Alongside the indispensable beasts of burden and draft animals, most farms probably also raised at least some poultry and smaller animals, which pastured on stony wasteland, in the woods, or sometimes on land left fallow. (But opinions differ on this matter.) They might also be fed leguminous plants and kitchen scraps. In many cases, this kind of stock-raising simply served to supplement the farm's produce. In others, where it was substantial and included cattle, there may have been veritable agropastoral farming. In the absence of informative sources, however, studies on the extent of combined farming remain at variance. Flocks inevitably posed the problem of how to feed them, and how to apportion land for pasturage and cultivation. On the whole, though with some exceptions, stock-raising was always the less important activity.

In certain regions, large herds of sheep and goats, of cattle, or, occasionally, of horses are attested. Often herds of sheep and goats, which were more mobile and more adaptable, would be moved over relatively short distances between the mountains, where they spent the summer, and the plains, where they remained for the winter. Alternatively, they might spend a few months on a small deserted island. Such transhumance is attested in particular by public conventions and agreements relating to the passage of flocks through neighboring cities or their temporary presence there, sometimes in return for the payment of a tax. Transgression of boundaries and disputes over pastures frequently gave rise to conflicts. A few landowners probably specialized in this type of extensive stock-raising. For example, according to two late third-century and early second-century-B.C. inscriptions (L. Migeotte, *L'emprunt public,* nos. 12 and 15), Eubolus of Elatea in Phocis owned at least two hundred twenty head of cattle and horses and a thousand sheep and goats, and we know of two female citizens of Copae in Boeotia, each of whom owned at least two hundred head of cattle and smaller livestock. These landowners must have possessed quite vast areas of pasturage with plentiful water, grass, and bushes, and must also have cultivated plants for fodder. In exchange for the payment of a due, they might also pasture their animals on the communal lands that are attested in a number of regions such as Arcadia and Boeotia. That is precisely the case recorded by the two inscriptions cited above, the first of which gave Eubolus the right of pasturage (*epinomia*) on the land of Orchomenus, in Boeotia. This text indicates that the sheep or goat flocks were five times as numerous as the herds of cattle and horses. No doubt the area was rich in pastureland.

Inscriptions in Delphi and Delos, for example, show further that certain sanctuaries used their land to raise animals. These are sometimes described as *hiera probata,* at least some of which (pigs, cattle, sheep) were probably destined for sacrifices. But such evidence is rare. Of course, stock-raising also provided supplies of milk, eggs, hides, and wool (sheep shearing took place in the spring), and these commodities, after processing, produced cheese, leather, textiles, and clothing. Both written sources and archaeological finds reveal the existence of stables and sheepfolds, and this presupposes the cultivation of fodder plants. But, since the climate made outdoor pasturage possible for much of the year and many stables were used to house plowing oxen, it is hard to calculate how many stables there were. The number certainly varied from one region to another and also depended on such other factors as the need to protect crops and trees from the voracity of goats and the availability of grazing ground, which diminished as cultivated areas expanded.

Beekeeping, Hunting, and Fishing

Beekeeping was widespread, for honey served as a sweetener and was used to make mead and medicaments. Hunting provided quite substantial supplies. Big game (deer, fallow deer, wild boar . . .) was mainly the prerogative of the rich, but small game (hares, rabbits, ducks, quails, woodcocks, pheasants, partridges, thrushes, larks, wood pigeons, plovers . . .) was within the grasp of all. These smaller animals were usually caught in traps. Farmers could supplement their diet by fishing, but there were also professional fishermen, who sometimes formed corporative groups. The sea produced fish (tuna, mackerel, swordfish, red mullet, sole, turbots, sardines, anchovies . . .), mollusks, and shellfish. The rivers, lakes, and marshes produced freshwater fish. The sea also provided sponges, salt (which was also mined), and murex (which was used to make purple dye).

FOODSTUFFS AND HOW THEY WERE USED

Barley and wheat, highly nutritious, were the staple food throughout antiquity. Mills and bakeries did exist, but in many small cities and above all out in the countryside, cereals were processed within the *oikos*. Wheat could be hulled by soaking and reduced to gruel, consumed as a kind of porridge. After milling and kneading, wheat was generally used to make bread (*artos*) with or without leaven, or else little cakes, dry or mixed with either cheese or honey. We know of various methods of cooking, but the stone oven made its hesitant appearance only in the Roman period, a fact that indicates a late date for the popularity of leavened wheaten bread. Barley could likewise be used to make bread, but it did not rise well and remained heavy.

For this reason it was usually toasted, then ground, producing a kind of flour (*alphita*), which was sold loose and could be preserved for as long as two or three months. It was used to make *maza,* the most common of basic staples, for which at least eight recipes are known to us, some involving cooking, others not. People often ate *maza* as a gruel to which water, milk, or honey could be added, but it could also be made into griddlecakes or rissoles. *Maza* was usually accompanied by some other food, known as *opson* (literally, "that which comes afterwards"): vegetables, olives, cheese, meat, fish, fruit, etc.

Olives filled a multiplicity of roles. They were an important source of nourishment, eaten raw, stuffed, or mashed. But above all they were used for oil. This was the material used for cooking or for preparing raw vegetables, sauces, and cakes. It also served for skin care (as oil to be applied after bathing or before exercising in the gymnasium), or it could be used in the preparation of perfumes or medicaments, or for other daily domestic purposes (lighting, lubrication, greasing wool, preserving clothing, etc.). As in the case of cereals, the processing of oil usually took place in the *oikos.*

Vegetables and leguminous plants were part of the daily diet and were served in a variety of local ways, often in soup, purées, or gruels, as an accompaniment to *maza* or even as a substitute for cereals. Similarly, much of the produce from hunting and fishing would be included in the daily diet. Some items, such as the eels from Lake Copaïs, in Boeotia, were considered luxury dishes. The meat of domesticated creatures, however, was consumed only on special occasions. These animals would be slaughtered in the context of a sacrifice, usually in the course of a festival or ceremony, after which the flesh and bones would be

ritually divided between men and the gods. The men's allot-
ment, that is to say the meat, would be shared out among those
present; the gods' share, the bones and fat, would be burned on
an altar, while the skins would usually be returned either to the
priests or to the city.

Wine was a common beverage, as was *kykeōn,* made from
barley gruel mixed with water and herbs. There were many different types of red, white, and rosé wine, the quality of which
varied from one region to another. (See, for example, Athenaeus,
The Deipnopsophists, I.51–72.) Many wines were consumed
locally and were of mediocre quality. Some households would
settle for drinking a second-rate wine made from marc and lees,
reserving their real wine for sale. But a few wines were famous .
(See below, p. 87.) An extremely refined recipe for Thasos wine
calls to mind the advice dispensed by Hesiod. (See above, p. 70.)
The recipe has come down to us via a tenth-century-A.D. text, no
doubt recording a traditional procedure. The grapes were
picked when they were perfectly ripe, exposed to the sun for five
days, then rinsed in a mixture of must and brine. They were
then left to stand for another day in the wine-pressing area, after
which they were trampled. Must reduced by boiling was then
added to the grape juice. After fermentation, this process produced highly alcoholic wine. It was then left to settle and rest in
large jars until the spring. The Greeks were clearly in the habit
of adding a variety of ingredients to their wine (salt water, herbs,
honey, spices such as cinnamon, and so on). They also made a
thick red wine that they drank diluted with water. A *kratēr*
would be used as a mixing bowl.

Food was thus relatively varied, although not equally so
everywhere, for it would depend on both a family's means and

also the local and regional resources. Nor was it the same in towns as in the countryside. For example, although wheaten bread became common in the Roman period, it was, in all probability, eaten only in cities.

CULTIVATING THE SOIL
Different Types of Property and Methods of Exploitation

As we have noted (p. 44), in the archaic period some of the land in mainland Greece and the Aegean area was progressively distributed among all or at least many of the citizens. A link was in principle clearly established between real estate and citizenship, even if some communities with inferior rights, like the *perioikoi* of Sparta, did retain their own land. In some cities landowner-ship even became a condition of citizenship. In these, each citi-zen's *klēros* or plot of land was held as an inalienable patrimony to be handed down from father to son. One such city was fifth-century Sparta, under the laws of Lycurgus. Here, every citizen owned a plot of land more or less equal to those of his fellow Spartans. Most other cities passed similar, if slightly less strict, laws governing inheritance, adoption, and the sale of plots of land. For both Plato and Aristotle, one of the primary condi-tions for an ideal city was a strict distribution of land among all the citizens, to be continued from one generation to the next.

The ideal of the citizen-landowner, whether of humble or average condition, remained inspirational for centuries and was actually realized in a number of instances. In fifth-century Attica, for which we possess a few figures, a good many citizens of hoplite rank (that is to say, men able to arm themselves and serve in the heavy infantry) owned allotments estimated to be roughly five hectares on average; if they needed to, they could rent additional plots of land. They would cultivate the land as a family group with a few slaves, both male and female, all work-ing together. Slaves helped the family both in the fields and in the house, particularly during the periods of harvesting and pro-cessing the crops, and they also looked after the livestock. Citizen-landowners might hire extra slaves or even landless and unemployed freemen, particularly for harvesting. In more or less every period, this type of *autourgos* (one who cultivated his land himself) was to be found everywhere, both in ancient cities, after the land had been divided up, and likewise in colonies or new cities that distributed the land equally right from the start.

A number of vaster properties nevertheless survived. Some calculations suggest that in the fifth century the large estates of Attica each comprised no more than 26 or 27 hectares and employed four or five permanent laborers. To us, this may seem quite modest, but at the time such a property would represent a fortune. In Thasos, large vine-growing estates seem to have cov-ered several dozen hectares. But since we possess few figures, estimates are inevitably fragile. It is, however, certain that, what with the difficulties of the time and changing *mores,* such large estates resumed from the fourth century onward, thereby undermining the old principle of the inalienability of patri-monies. In this respect, Attica was affected less than some other regions. At this time it included a number of properties of sev-eral dozen hectares, and, according to some estimates, one-third or one-quarter of its cultivated land may have belonged to no more than two thousand citizens, barely one-tenth of the civic population. But elsewhere this trend was even more marked, particularly in the Peloponnese. (See above, p. 45.) From the second century B.C. onward, it gathered pace everywhere, for at this point most cities in effect passed under the domination of oligarchs whose wealth consisted essentially of real estate. These rich landowners clearly delegated the management of their estates to stewards (*epitropoi* or *epistatai*), often of servile status (see Xenophon, *Oeconomicus* XII) and entrusted the care of their land and livestock to a labor force probably composed of free peasants as well as slaves.

As has been noted in chapter 1 (p. 41), a third, very different farming system also existed. It took a variety of forms and was practiced not only in European Greece and the islands but also in the new cities founded in the archaic and the Hellenistic periods. Here, the land was cultivated by indigenous peoples who lived in villages at some distance from the urban centers. These communities, which were collectively dependent on the cities, paid the landowners dues or a tribute, frequently a percentage of their harvests. The best-known of such cases are Sparta and Crete, where the dependents' contributions were used to provide communal meals for the citizens (Plutarch, *Life of Lycurgus* 12.1–10: Austin and Vidal-Naquet, no. 57). Some such properties were quite vast, probably several dozen hectares. In Sparta, the average area of a fifth-century *klēros* ranged from 10 to 18 hectares, that is to say twice or three times the size of an average Athenian *klēros* of the same period. However, the appropriation of extra land became rife in Sparta, and, in the following century, the situation there was far graver than it was in Athens. (See above, p. 45.)

There were also public and sacred estates. Literary and, above all, epigraphical sources refer to many such examples, in Athens, in Thespiae, in the islands (Delos, Rhenea, Myconos, Thasos, Ceos, Chios, Amorgos), in several cities in Caria, and in Lucanian

Heraclea, among other places. In fact, it seems that every city, however modest, included at least a few estates of this kind. It has been estimated that in Attica, in the classical period, such areas (half of which were the property of demes) represented roughly one- tenth of the land suitable for cultivation. In the Hellenistic period, Apollo was the largest landowner in the Cyclades, owning land and houses on Delos and the neighboring islands of Myconos and Rhenea. As time passed, estates of this kind even tended to multiply everywhere, as a result of seizures and confiscations or gifts from benefactors (*euergetai*). Such plots of land and farms were generally leased to individuals who tendered for them. Many of the leases that have come down to us record not only the leasing conditions but also a number of interesting recommendations concerning crops, the upkeep of the land, and the state in which it was to be returned when the contract expired. Most such leases were based on a previous model contract. For instance, we know of the *hiera syngraphē,* literally the "sacred contract," of Delos, a document of 300 B.C., which established the general rules to be followed when leasing out land and houses belonging to the sanctuary. In particular, we learn that leases for agricultural land had to be auctioned every ten years, while leases for houses were auctioned every five years. These documents show that estate management was generally conservative. Most of the tenants were wealthy citizens who complemented their own patrimony in this fashion for a while, thereby increasing their incomes. Nowhere do these leases appear to have been used to help small-scale landowners or to provide land for citizens who lacked it. In the Hellenistic East, there were also sacred estates, no doubt vast, about which little is known. These were cultivated by village populations and sacred slaves.

The Organization and Occupation of the Land

From the archaic period onward, in European Greece and the Aegean islands, all the useful land was progressively occupied. Cultivation won out over stock-raising, which appears to have been more widespread in earlier centuries. Valleys and good land suited to cultivation were relatively hard to find, however. According to Thucydides (I.2.3), the best land for cereals lay in Thessaly, Boeotia, and the Peloponnese with the exception of Arcadia. There was also some to be found on the islands (Lemnos, Melos, Samos, Thasos . . .), in Ionia, Cilicia, Sicily, Cyrenaïca, and along the shores of the Black Sea. Thus after the emigrations of the archaic period and in response to the demographic peaking of the fifth century, new land had to be acquired by "internal colonization." Surveys carried out in several regions of mainland Greece (Attica, Boeotia, Argolis, Thessaly), in southern Italy and Sicily, and in the islands of Thasos, Ceos, Chios, and Delos, among others, indicate intensive occupation of the land from the archaic period down to the first half of the Hellenistic period, although there were certainly local variants and fluctuations during that time. Thus, from the fourth century B.C. onward, isolated farmsteads multiplied, except in Attica, where grouped settlements persisted. The example of Thasos, with its urban center, its forests, its villages in the valleys, its numerous scattered farmsteads, and its network of roads, indicates a dense, tightly knit community, intensive exploitation of the territory, and a close symbiosis between town and countryside.

Recent surveys in many regions, in particular the Aegean islands, have revealed on the slopes of hills and mountains terraces dating from the fifth century (and on Delos, even from the sixth). Such projects (involving land clearance, excavation, the construction of supporting walls, and embanking) must have been very time-consuming and required a large labor force, but in the long run they paid off. Quite apart from extending the area of arable land, terraces made it possible to save the rain that fell between autumn and spring and to limit erosion. Furthermore, as Plato explained in *The Laws* (VI, 761a–b), water could thus be captured, stored in tanks and cisterns, and then distributed among the fields and the inhabited settlements via ditches and canals. Such arrangements have rarely been found in the Greek world, but recently some have been identified on the islands of Tenos and Delos. Other means of irrigation, drawing on rivers, springs, and wells, were frequently employed even on low-lying land, at least over limited areas. Certain marshy plains were drained, in particular in parts of the Peloponnese and in Eretria in Euboea and Larissa in Thessaly. The draining of Lake Copaïs, in Boeotia, started at an early date, was resumed in Alexander's time, and continued right down to the second century A.D., although it was never completed. On low-lying land, stones frequently had to be cleared and were then used to erect low walls marking out separate plots of land, to border roads, and to prevent flocks from straying into cultivated areas. All such work clearly involved communal efforts, in which everyone was expected to collaborate and in which the city itself would often play a leading role or provide the initiative. It would then see that the irrigation structures were respected and well maintained and that water was not wasted.

As for heaths, wasteland, and woods, mostly situated in the mountainous regions or on the edges (*eschatiai*) of agricultural

estates and civic territories, these were used for grazing livestock, beekeeping, hunting and gathering, and collecting wood
and charcoal supplies. Many such spaces constituted common,
public, or sacred land.

In many parts of European Greece and the islands, occupation of the land began to decline around 200 B.C. At this point
many rural sites disappeared, and parts of the countryside were
deserted. This exodus favored the growth of some towns, while
others withered away. Large estates multiplied in the hands of
the wealthy, who employed a large workforce composed of both
slaves and freemen. Some agriculture became speculative, prior-
itizing the cultivation of vines or trees on the best land, but on
the whole it regressed, giving way to extensive stock-raising.
Large flocks would graze over quite vast tracts of land, appar-
ently paying scant attention to city frontiers. The causes of this
phenomenon are complex. Wars with their attendant requisi-
tioning and destruction (see above, p. 24), encouraging banditry
and creating insecurity, undoubtedly played a major role. As for
the demographic slump (see above, p. 22), whether it was a cause
or a consequence of the decline is hard to say. A degree of recovery is perceptible at the beginning of the empire, for example in
the Peloponnese, where renewed rural activity is detectable. But
even the efforts of emperors were unable to reverse the trend.
Small or medium-sized agricultural concerns, about which we
know virtually nothing, must have survived. But much of the
land was now in the hands of elite groups, some extremely rich,
and many of them Romanized. These were inclined to invest in
cattle raising and also horse breeding, to stock their stables. The
best-known example of such a member of the elite is Herodes
Atticus, in Athens in the second century A.D.

Asia Minor also suffered from the events of the late Hellenistic period. But it could rely on more numerous and more diverse resources; and by the beginning of the empire it had recovered. Many of its cities were rich and prosperous. As in European Greece, many traditional types of farming endured, particularly in the west. But great estates cultivated by tribute-paying and dependent peasants also multiplied, to the profit of the rich landowners, who now included Romans. Landowning aristocracies established themselves in places such as the Black Sea area and Cappadocia. There were also a number of imperial estates that were worked by indigenous peoples. The Greek world never produced any equivalent to the great Italian *latifundia*, however.

SELF-SUFFICIENCY AND MARKETS

Although methods of cultivation and stock-raising remained stable for centuries and diverse kinds of property management operated in all periods, the cultivation of the soil did undergo profound development, and this speeded up from the late Hellenistic period onward. As in other societies, a desire for self-sufficiency and dependable subsistence was characteristic of cultivators who worked their own land (*autourgoi*). This remained the dominant model from the eighth down to the third century B.C. throughout the Greek world, at the level of every *oikos* and above all of every city. Most cultivators had from time immemorial practiced a mixed agriculture, combining a number of different crops and at least a little stock-raising. They deployed systematic efforts to obtain the greatest possible yield from their land and to diversify their cultivation of foodstuffs. They stored a reserve of provisions sufficient to cover several years, in case of poor harvests, suggesting that in normal conditions they produced more than they actually needed. Furthermore, to minimize the risks of bad weather and disease, in general they favored dispersed plots of land rather than a single one. It has been established that five hectares, three of which were devoted to cereals, along with a little stock-raising and around sixty olive trees, sufficed to feed a family. Even in early times, however, *oikoi* within the same territory, which stuck by one another since they all suffered from the same constraints, did trade a proportion of what they produced in local markets, making the two activities complementary at the level of the city. Moreover, self-sufficiency as it was understood in practice also entailed external trading. (See above, pp. 34–35.) It seems, then, that many cities managed to be self-sufficient, at least in the essentials and by dint of regional trading. It has recently been shown, for example, that the Cyclades and other small Aegean islands were self-sufficient in this sense between 500 and 200 B.C., despite the fact that classical (particularly Athenian) literature represented them as arid and poverty-stricken.

There were, however, other modes of behavior. According to Plutarch (*Life of Pericles* 16), Pericles was the first to run his *oikos* as a kind of business. Hard pressed for time as he was, he found it more convenient to sell his entire stock of agricultural produce (rather than set aside part of it for subsistence) and then repair to the market to buy whatever he needed. He kept strict records of his expenses and receipts, imposing upon his household an austere way of life that was little appreciated. In the early Hellenistic period, the Aristotelian author of the *Oeconomica,* the second treatise on economics that has come down to us, cited, as a well-known model, the *oikonomia Attikē,* the Athenian way of managing one's *oikos.* He summarized this as follows: "as one sells, one buys," going on to say that the smallest agricultural concerns had no need even for a cellar or a storehouse (1344b31–33 and 1345a17–19). This management method was clearly oriented toward selling produce in the market. We do not know to what extent it was adopted in Attica, but it was no doubt considered there to be "modern."

Depending on the options afforded by their land and their personal methods, some landowners practiced a speculative kind of agriculture, specializing in particular products destined for export. Already in the archaic and classical periods this was not unknown, although we do not know its extent. In many regions the trend intensified from the fourth century B.C. onward, without, however, eliminating self-sufficient farming, and never, it seems, going as far as monoculture. Economic development thus took place in tandem with the political and social events that were raising up oligarchies of prominent citizens everywhere. Despite inevitable highs and lows, most of those specializations enjoyed a long life, as numerous examples show. A number are worth citing. Thasos, Lesbos, Chios, and Rhodes produced well-known wines, whose production and exportation were carefully organized. Situated close to the vineyards of Thasos and Rhodes were workshops producing the amphoras in which the wine was exported. Most wines produced in the islands, and those of Mende, Maronea, Ionia, Lydia, and Caria, were also of high quality. Agrigentum too not only boasted vast, excellent vineyards, but also exported oil to Carthage. Athens was famous for its oil (as was Samos), its honey (as were the Cyclades), and its figs. Megara was known for its vegetables, Boeotia for its grain, fish, and game, the islands of Cythnos and Ceos for their cheeses, and Thessaly, Thrace, Cilicia, Cappadocia, and Armenia for their horses. Meanwhile Thessaly, the Black Sea coast, Sicily, and Cyrenaïca were all noted for their grain, Marseilles for its wine and oil, Cyzicus, Sinope, and other northern cities for their dried and salted fish. The Black Sea coast of Asia Minor was famous for its wood, its pitch and resin, and its flax and hemp. Phrygia, Galatia, and Cappadocia were all famous for their wool, and many other regions of Asia Minor were renowned for their figs, walnuts, hazelnuts, dried fruit (apples, pears, and cherries), and for their dyes and spices, among other things.

Speculative farming was marked by a mercantile spirit, which is even more noticeable in the craft industries and commerce. (See below, pp. 98–99 and 138–40.) Those two domains both achieved varying levels of success and developed along the same lines as agriculture.

PRIMARY TEXTS

The Oikonomia, *Agriculture, and Craft Industries as Seen by an Athenian of the Fourth Century* B.C.

Well now, we thought that estate management is the name of a branch of knowledge, and this knowledge appeared to be that by which men can increase estates, and an estate appeared to be identical with the total of one's property, and we said that property is that which is useful for supplying a livelihood, and useful things turn out to be all those things that one knows how to use. Now we thought that it is impossible to learn all the sciences, and we agreed with our states in rejecting the so-called illiberal arts, because they seem to spoil the body and unnerve the mind. . . . We came to the conclusion that for a gentleman the best occupation and the best science is husbandry, from which men obtain what is necessary to them. For this occupation seemed to be the easiest to learn and the pleasantest to work at, to give the body the greatest measure of strength and beauty, and to leave to the mind the greatest amount of spare time for attending to the interests of one's friends and city. Moreover, since the crops grow and the cattle on a farm graze outside the walls, husbandry seemed to us to help in some measure to make the workers valiant. And so this way of making a living appeared to be held in the highest estimation by our states, because it seems to turn out the best citizens and the most loyal to the community.

> Xenophon, *Oeconomicus* VI.4–10, translated by E. C.
> Marchant, The Loeb Classical Library, 1965

Contract for the Leasing of Land Belonging to Zeus Temenites by the City of Arkesine in Amorgos (Mid-fourth Century B.C.)

The lessee . . . will furnish the temple administrators with suitable sureties . . . of the whole rent, and will pay the rent in the month of Thargelion every year, free of all taxes. If he fails to pay there shall be exacted from the lessee and his sureties a fine equivalent to half the rent.

He will plough half the land each year, and not all the land in a single year. If he ploughs fallow land there will be three ploughings. He will dig round the vines twice, first in Anthesterion and again before the twentieth of Taureon, and round the fig trees once. If he fails to do this according to the lease agreement he will pay a fine of an obol for each vine or fig tree round which he fails to dig, and three drachmas for each *zugon* he fails to plough.

The sureties must guarantee the whole payment of the rent and of all required additional work, if the lessee wishes to retain possession; otherwise the temple administrators are to rent it out again.

He will build up again at his own expense all walls that are falling down; if he does not build them up, let him pay a fine of a drachma per *orguia* [= about two meters]. He will strengthen all the walls along the road and leave them strengthened when he vacates the land.

Each year he will apply 150 measures of manure with a basket holding 1 *medimnos* and 4 *hemiekta*. If he does not apply it he will pay a fine of three obols per basket shortfall. He will make a pledge to the temple administrators that he has applied the manure according to the lease agreement.

He will keep the roofs watertight, and hand them over in this condition. The vines that are cut off the temple administrators must sell.

He will dig the ditches in the month Eiraphion, in the places marked out by the temple administrators, four-foot ones and three-foot ones, and will put in the plants in the presence of the temple administrators, planting twenty vines at the spacing ordered by the temple administrators, and ten fig trees, and he will build an additional wall above the land.

He will provide security consisting of storage jars, if the wall is not built, and the lessee will make a pledge to the temple administrators.

If he does not plant the plants, let him pay a fine of a drachma per plant shortfall.

No one shall be allowed to bring flocks into the sanctuary; if anyone does bring them in, the flocks are to be sacred to Zeus Temenites. Anyone who wishes can make an indication to the council and be rewarded with half.

If the temple administrators want to plant additional fig trees . . . , they may do so.

When the farmer vacates the land, let him leave behind 150 loads of manure and let him measure it out before the temple administrators with a basket containing a *medimnos* and 4 *hemiekta*. If he does not measure it out, let him pay a drachma per basket shortfall. Let the temple administrators exact the fine or themselves owe double.

He will dig a trench around the fallow land. If he does not dig a trench round it let him pay twenty drachmas. Let him hand over . . . at the same time as the rent.

Let him hand over . . . , whatever is of the year, to the treasurers in the month Thargelion separately from the rent. If he does not hand it over, let him be liable to a fine equal to half of the treasures.

Anything that is subject to dispute the temple administrators along with the farmer (?) are to sell in the agora to whoever bids most, or themselves pay double. Anyone who wishes may indicate them before the *masteres* and be rewarded with half.

If he plants and leaves . . . if not, he will pay . . . for each fathom.

Translated by P. J. Rhodes and R. Osborne,
Greek Historical Inscriptions 404–323 B.C.,
no. 59 (Oxford, 2003)

THREE

Craft Industries
and Business Ventures

The double title of this chapter is designed to cover a wide spectrum of activities of varying scale, ranging from small workshops to large businesses, with one feature in common to all: they all involved the transformation of natural products into finished articles. The usual Greek word for these activities was *technai,* a term that could apply to the fine arts as well as to craftsmanship and also designated various professional and intellectual activities. These *technai* were linked on the one hand with agriculture, which provided many of the raw materials that the *technai* processed, and on the other hand with commerce, since many of their products were destined for the marketplace, where they were sold by the craftsmen who had produced them. Most of these businesses were privately owned, in many cases by foreigners who had personally set them up. Citizens seldom attempted to regulate them by law. But in some cases the cities themselves owned workshops or businesses and were, above all, the initiators of large-scale projects.

Many literary and epigraphical texts refer to these activities, and they are portrayed by the iconography of painted vases. Archaeological excavations have uncovered not only a mass of fabricated objects but also the remains of workshops, entire town quarters dedicated to craft industries, and public construction sites. Notwithstanding this abundance of evidence, our knowledge of the different sectors, regions, and periods is very uneven. We know more about public works than about private craftsmanship. Although these activities have been the subject of many artistic and technical studies, they are here presented from an economic point of view, that is to say, as a sector of production.

PRIVATE CRAFTS
Their Evolution and Scale

Many *technai* clearly appeared very early on. By the Bronze Age they were diversifying to produce not only food, living quarters, clothing, equipment, weapons, and tools, but also a mass of products needed in daily life. The rate at which development took place escapes us, but it was certainly not continuous, since it depended on the size and the needs of local communities. But from the archaic period onwards, demographic growth, the progress of urbanization, and the diversification of needs led to a multiplication of trades. Already in the classical period, many specializations appear in the urban centers. In Athens, one of the most highly developed towns, texts make it possible to identify about one hundred different manual trades, all linked to the production of material goods. It also appears that, quite apart from metics and slaves, ten thousand of the thirty to forty thousand Athenian citizens worked in this sector. In the Hellenistic and imperial periods, specialized trades were at least as numerous in the most active towns, to judge by the wide variety of professional associations and trades that are mentioned in epitaphs. Many of these texts come from Asia Minor, where urbanization was in full swing.

Without imposing assumptions as to how they were organized, we can form some idea of the variety of trades by grouping them into different categories: the preparation of foodstuffs (e.g., millers, bakers, grocers, butchers, fishmongers), work with stone (e.g., quarrymen, marble masons, stone cutters, chiselers, engravers), work with wood (e.g., carpenters, joiners, cabinetmakers, sculptors), work with metal (e.g., blacksmiths, workers with bronze, goldsmiths), work with clay (e.g., potters, painters, tile and brick makers), work with skins and leather (e.g., tanners, curriers, cobblers, saddlers, harness makers), work with textiles (e.g., fullers, dyers, weavers, tailors, embroiderers, carpet makers); and the list should also include makers of musical instruments, perfumers, glassblowers, and so on. Working together in the same field or the same workshop, craftsmen and manual workers would master several techniques and be competent to perform a variety of tasks. Meanwhile, as early as the classical period, architects, sculptors, vase-painters, and even teams of potters and blacksmiths moved from one workshop to another, wherever there was a demand for their skills. That mobility indicates a degree of competition, at least in the quest for quality. In a text that is often cited (see below, p. 114; Austin and Vidal-Naquet, no. 6B), Xenophon explained how the division of trades improved the quality of products, and Plato noted that it also enabled increased production (*Republic* II, 870c).

The volume of craft industries in the economy is impossible to assess, but it certainly counted for less than agriculture and employed a far smaller workforce. In the vast majority of communities, material needs were limited, and many could be satisfied by work within the family *oikos*. Furthermore, as in the domain of agriculture, cities aspired to self-sufficiency in *technai*. In general, supplies adapted to demand. Conditions thus did not much favor economic competition, of which, indeed, there is little sign. Most producers seem to have been very cautious.

Many fabricated products and most of the construction work and the monuments can undoubtedly be rated technical successes. The level of skills, the ability to make accurate calculations, and the quality of tools and know-how were all clearly high and had not suffered from any technological block. (See above, pp. 18–21.) Indeed, architects, artists, and craftsmen often displayed considerable originality. All the same, forms and styles evolved slowly, over centuries, and adaptations and personal choices generally stayed within well-established concepts, plans, and canons. In this domain too, clearly, tradition and conservatism weighed extremely heavily.

Workplaces

The rural *oikos* was always one place where the products of agriculture, stock-raising, foraging, and woodcutting were processed. The most taxing tasks (milling grain, crushing and pressing olives, treading grapes, soaking and fulling hides, and preparing charcoal, e.g.) were frequently assigned to male slaves. Other tasks generally fell to women, whether free or slaves: it was they who kneaded flour; cooked bread and cakes; carded, spun and wove wool and flax; braided wicker, rushes, and reeds; and prepared dyes. Cultivators liked to make and repair their own tools and to construct and maintain their own farm buildings. All these activities, regarded as typically domestic, were an integral part of agricultural life. They contributed to self-sufficiency, even if certain products were sold outside the *oikos*. They were clearly unable, however, to provide for the growing and increasingly diverse needs of urban settlements.

A craftsman's workshop was specialized by definition, but it would also serve as a shop. It was usually known as an *ergastērion,* a "workplace." These were often handed down from father to son, and we know of a number of dynasties of both artists and sculptors. If the boss owned the workshop, he had to be a citizen. Many metics were therefore leaseholders, although the city might grant the right to own property to a rare few. Most *ergastēria* employed at least a few workers, either freemen or slaves, usually chosen on the basis of family links or dependence on the master. Free and slave workers frequently performed the same tasks. Indeed, although slaves were used above all for purely manual labor, there were some among the craftsman's apprentices or pupils. In large or small towns, many workshops were set up either in a family home, where they might occupy a couple of rooms, or else in a public place such as an agora or a portico, where premises could be rented. Sometimes they would be clustered together in particular quarters of the town, like the "industrial quarter" to the southwest of the Athenian agora in the direction of Piraeus, or they might be sited out beyond the town walls, where their noise could not cause a nuisance and prevailing winds would carry away their smells and smoke. There were also workshops situated in the countryside within easy reach of the raw materials they needed and roads to transport them.

Apart from regulations concerning the siting of workshops and taxation, public interventions into the domain of craft industries seem to have been limited. The "stamping" of many tiles and amphoras—in particular the amphoras transporting wine from Thasos, Rhodes, Cnidus, Cos, Sinope, and Heraclea on the Black Sea—no doubt testifies to some form of administrative control. Many of these marks stamped into clay incorporate various emblems and figures, and two proper names, of which it seems that one was a magistrate's, possibly the city agoranome's. (On this one, see below, p. 144.) A number of scholars interpret this as a sign of a tax levied on the product, but conclusive evidence on this score is lacking. Near several sanctuaries, archaeological excavations have found traces of metallurgical workshops producing votive objects. It is not certain whether these workshops were situated within the sacred precinct, as were the shops of the Heraion of Samos, for example. (See below, p. 148.) No extant text mentions communal grain or oil mills, such as can be found in other civilizations. It should be noted, finally, that since the Greeks had no legal notion of communal responsibility, a workshop had no juridical identity as such: the law recognized only individuals.

Different Types of Production

Workshops varied considerably in size. Most were quite modest, producing cheap, useful articles for local customers or the local market. We do not know much about them, but the owner and his family must have operated some. Others might hire or buy a few workers, though slaves represented a considerable investment of capital. These people worked to order and did not store any stock. They made up the majority of *banausoi,* and, even if their products were appreciated, they themselves, as a social group, were not much respected. (See above, pp. 31–33.)

Other workshops employed more workers and did not necessarily limit themselves to the local market. They might specialize in more up-market trades such as the production of luxury clothing, purple dyeing, preparing and engraving stelae or inscribing monuments (increasingly in demand in many cities), or, under the direction of "masters," they might produce artistic items (painted ceramics, stone or bronze sculptures, and so forth). These did win respect, thanks to the refinement and costliness of their products. Prices varied according to the quality, reputation, or rarity of the products and to labor and transport costs, in other words with the law of supply and demand.

Certain workshops constituted veritable businesses, run on a much larger scale. These were always less numerous but multiplied from the Hellenistic period on. Athenian literature of the classical period provides a number of often-cited examples: Cephalus's shield factory, which employed one hundred twenty slaves (Lysias, *Against Eratosthenes* 19); Demosthenes' father's two factories, which produced knives and beds, employing thirty and twenty workers, respectively; the orator said (*Against Aphobus* I.9) that neither was a "small affair" (*mikra technē*), for they brought in, respectively, 3,000 and 12,000 drachmas a year. We hear of the flour mill of Nausicydes, Cyrebus's bakery, Demeas's cloak factory and that of Meno, producing coats of fine wool, to which Xenophon alludes in his *Memorabilia* (II.7.6), among others. In the domain of textiles, the chitons of Megara and the woolen cloth and clothes of Miletus were much prized in the classical and Hellenistic periods. Several regions of western Asia Minor favored sheep-raising, the cultivation of flax and hemp, and the fabrication of textiles, clothing, carpets, and ropes. Many of these businesses were situated in the well-watered valleys of the Hermus and Maeander rivers, where much evidence dating from the Hellenistic and Roman periods has been found. In the agricultural sector, it is worth picking out Thasos from among the many examples cited above (see pp. 87–88): Thasos possessed vineyards several dozen hectares in area and workshops producing amphoras. There were also private businesses that required diverse machinery and equipment as well as cooperation between several different trades: tile manufacturing, salt, iron and copper mines, logging, clay and stone quarrying, shipbuilding, and so on. In this domain, the sources (see below) mention only a few public projects.

Our sources do not describe these businesses. Most were probably not really large factories, but rather collective projects, directed by managers and involving a number of small workshops scattered here and there in the towns or set up in private *oikoi*. These may have employed a larger servile workforce than workshops operated in isolation. Their products were destined not solely for local markets, but for neighboring regions and distant clients as well. Some of their prices were high, above all those for luxury products such as textiles and clothing of fine linen or silk; but they fluctuated in response to the law of supply and demand. The proprietors of such businesses were rich, some of them extremely so. Some of those in Asia Minor owned large herds and flocks as well as numerous workshops.

PUBLIC WORKS

Cities and sanctuaries often undertook works of common interest. These were linked, more or less directly, with either public or sacred property. Some of them involved large, costly building sites requiring heavy materials and a large workforce, specialized or not. Sometimes the cities and sanctuaries themselves managed these projects, but in many cases they entrusted the execution to private entrepreneurs.

Quarries

There were many stone quarries, which were generally either public or sacred property. In Athens, some were owned by demes. In Ephesus, they belonged to Artemis. An inscription dating from around 200 B.C., from an unidentified city, mentions public revenues from stone (*apo lithōn*), no doubt referring to the sale of stone extracted from the city's quarries (L. Migeotte, *L'emprunt public,* no. 118). In the Hellenistic period, many quarries were owned by kings and then became imperial property under Augustus. Although we are quite well informed about their techniques of extraction and sawing and also about their means of transport both by sea and overland, little is known about their labor forces, which must have been both large and diversified. Quarries supplied one of the indispensable materials for constructions of many kinds, both private and public: marble was crucial for large buildings and monuments in particular. The marbles of Paros, Thasos, Naxos, and Athens (Hymettus and Pentelicus) were among those most highly valued.

Ochre was greatly in demand on account of its pharmaceutical uses and, above all, as a coating for the prows of triremes (warships with three levels of oarsmen). In the first half of the fourth century B.C., Athens for the second time commandeered all exports of red ochre from the island of Ceos. (See below, pp. 168–69.)

Forestry

Some forests were privately owned; others, no doubt the larger ones, were situated on land owned by cities or sanctuaries, or else within royal or imperial estates. They certainly varied greatly in both size and importance. Wood was used, among other things, for manufacturing furniture and also for statues. Pine, fir, and cedar wood, in particular, were used for the roof-joists of buildings or the prows and masts of ships, two sectors in which cities, kings, and emperors were the biggest clients. The workers' felling, splitting, and sawing techniques are well known, as are the means of transport overland (hauling, wagon loads) and by water (floating, rafts, boats). Athens procured most of its supplies of wood from Macedonia. (See below, pp. 161–62.) But southern Italy, Thrace, Crete, Cyprus, and several regions of Asia Minor (the Troad, Mysia, Bithynia, Caria, Lycia, Cilicia Trachea, and others) were also rich in dense forests. Major logging projects clearly needed large workforces. In 399, Dionysius of Syracuse sent a large contingent of woodcutters to Etna, at that time densely covered with pines and firs, and another to Italy, from which he had obtained the right to export wood. The wood was dragged to the seacoast by draft animals and transported from there on rafts guided by ships all the way to

Syracuse (Diodorus Siculus, XIV.42). In 315/4, the king of Macedon, Antigonus the One-eyed, had a fleet built in Rhodes, Cilicia, and Phoenicia. The shipyard in Cilicia used wood from the Taurus mountain range, and those in Phoenicia used the famous cedars of Lebanon, where 8,000 men felled the trees and sawed up the wood, which was then transported to the coast by 1,000 teams of draft animals (Diodorus Siculus, XIX.58).

Mines (Metalla)

Seams of iron and copper were probably mined by private individuals, but little is known about them. Iron deposits were far more plentiful than copper, which was, however, found in Thrace and also on the islands of Cythnos and Cyprus. Gold and silver mines were also rare, but were more precious, so we know more about them. Most were public property, like the two examples described below. At the end of the sixth century, the mines of Siphnos enriched the Siphnians, who shared out the profits among themselves every year (Herodotus, III.57: Austin and Vidal-Naquet, no. 20A).

THE THRACIAN MINES

Thrace was famous in antiquity not only for its rich soil and forests but, above all, for its mines of gold and silver in the region of Mount Pangaeum. Several seams there had been mined, probably for many years, by the indigenous population (Herodotus, VII.112). Thasos possessed gold mines over and above those on the island itself and also several trading ports along the coast, from which it derived so much revenue that it imposed no taxes on its citizens' agricultural produce. In total, its annual income amounted to as much as 200 or even 300 talents (Herodotus, VI.46: Austin and Vidal-Naquet, no. 94). The Athenians had taken an interest in the region ever since the sixth century B.C. In 476, they founded a trading center (*emporion*) at Eïon, close to the mouth of the river Strymon, and then (in 437) a colony (*apoikia*) a little further north, at Amphipolis. This enabled them to control trade with the interior (Thucydides, IV.102.1–4). In 465 a conflict broke out between Athens and Thasos over the *emporia* and the mining sector Thasos was exploiting on the mainland. In 463 Thasos was obliged to hand everything over to Athens (Thucydides, I.100.2 and 101.3). In 422, during the Peloponnesian War, Amphipolis fell into the hands of the Spartan Brasidas. Between 410 and 407, Thasos began to regain its footing on the mainland. In the fourth century, Philip of Macedon infiltrated the region in his turn, capturing Amphipolis in 357. He then extended and refounded the town of Crenides, naming it Philippi. He so intensified exploitation of the mines in the *chōra* that they provided him with a revenue of over a thousand talents or six million drachmas (Diodorus Siculus, XVI.8.6). As Philippi was an autonomous city, it may be that the king simply obtained a mining concession there and did not himself own the mines. He probably also secured the Thracian mines of Mount Pangaeum, thanks to which he was able to mint many gold coins. These mines remained royal property until, under the Roman Empire, all the Thracian mines became part of the imperial estate. Their administration was organized by procurators, who leased them to private entrepreneurs.

This example and the one that follows give us a clear idea of how highly coveted these types of resources were, and show that cities and states had powerful reasons for appropriating them.

Thucydides (IV.105.1) mentions that he himself possessed certain rights of exploitation in the gold mines not far from Amphipolis; and some scholars have concluded that he had inherited them from his Thracian ancestors. The text, however, really appears to refer to a concession (*ktēsis ergasias*) rather than an actual property.

THE LAURION MINES

These mines of silver-bearing lead had been worked as early as the fourteenth century B.C., in the Mycenaean period, and may have been exploited even earlier, initially at surface level and later using underground galleries. They continued to be worked constantly right down to the first century B.C. when they became exhausted, but it was in the classical period that their yield peaked. In the region of Thorikos, in southeastern Attica, excavations have revealed a complex and well-equipped "industrial center": underground galleries where the ore was extracted, workshops and kilns for grading, crushing, and fusing it. The fact that such installations were costly and permanent suggests that they must have belonged to the citizens who owned the land above ground and who, according to the lease conditions, were obliged to allow miners access to the underground galleries and the workshops. Mining operations required abundant supplies of water and wood as well as a large workforce of both freemen and slaves. It has often been estimated, on the basis of Thucydides (VII.27.5: Austin and Vidal-Naquet, no. 76), that the number of slaves employed was in excess of twenty thousand, but this text actually describes the loss of the whole Attic countryside in 413–410 and the enemy's acquisition of slaves from every part of it, many of whom were craftsmen (*cheirotechnai*).

All the same, slaves certainly were preponderant in the work-force of the Laurion mines, and it was they who were assigned the hardest tasks, extraction of the ore in particular. Sometime before 413, Nicias rented out a thousand slaves, for one obol per head per day, to a Thracian manager whom he had probably himself bought and then freed (Xenophon, *Poroi* IV.14). During the Peloponnesian War, many slaves took flight, and the enemy occupation dealt a severe blow to mining.

The Laurion mines belonged to the city of Athens and brought it considerable wealth. Indeed, they were one of the bases of its power in the classical period. Drawing on figures gleaned from our sources, many attempts have been made to estimate their yield. According to Herodotus (VII.144: Austin and Vidal-Naquet, no. 20B), when, in 483, new seams increased the public revenue, the Athenians were at first keen on dividing up this manna at the rate of ten drachmas per head (no doubt per year, like the Siphnians). Themistocles, however, persuaded them to devote it instead to the construction of a fleet of warships. In *The Athenian Constitution* (22.7), Aristotle (or one of his disciples) alludes to the same event and notes that the revenue amounted to one hundred talents.

The mines were distributed as concessions to private individuals, who had to bid for them for a specified number of years, three in some cases (Aristotle, *The Athenian Constitution* 47.2), in others for longer periods (seven or ten years, depending on interpretations). Scholars have reconstructed thirty-nine different inscriptions referring to three hundred leases strung out over sixty years or more, between 367/6 and about 300 (Austin and Vidal-Naquet, no. 95). These texts, which are both lacunose and elliptical, have given rise to numerous contradictory interpretations from which it is hard to draw any firm conclusions. The number of mines was high and fluctuated from one period to another. A recent estimate suggests five hundred at the time of their most intense exploitation, around the mid-fourth century; but that figure may be exaggerated. The mines were classified into four categories: the old, the new, and two doubtless intermediary categories, the definitions of which are disputed. The inscriptions still display several dozen legible sums, all in round figures, most of which (80 percent) vary between 20 and 150 drachmas, but their significance remains unclear: perhaps they refer to rents or taxes strung out over longer or shorter periods. Attempts have also been made to estimate the volume of silver produced and the annual profit made by the city, but the results of these attempts, too, are widely divergent. We do not even know on what basis the city took or reserved the proportion of silver for the minting of coins and the fabrication of such precious objects as sacred vases: According to an entry in the *Suda,* a tenth-century-A.D. work that seems to refer to Athens, those who exploited the mines had to provide the city with a proportion of the ore (one:twenty-fourth, to be precise). The text does not, unfortunately, indicate to what period this refers.

In good periods, the mines also enriched certain individuals. Nicias made roughly ten talents annually from renting out his slaves, and the sum that he left at his death was estimated at the huge total of 100 talents, or 600,000 drachmas (Lysias, *On the Property of Aristophanes* 47). The sale of the silver and the lead too (Pseudo-Aristotle, *Oeconomica* 1353a15–18) could likewise be very profitable. We know that some individuals invested sums on the order of 2,000 to 9,000 drachmas in the mines (Demosthenes, *Against Nausimachus and Xenopeithes* 22 and *Against Boeotus* II.52). It would seem that this type of investment was accessible only to the wealthy. Thanks to a de facto monopoly, not only were the overwhelming majority of concession-holders citizens, but the wealthiest played a preponderant role: this provides some indication of their spirit of free enterprise.

Public Constructions

In every period cities, at their own cost, erected, maintained, and restored many infrastructures (ports, wharves, warehouses, arsenals, markets, streets, roads, fountains, cisterns, and so forth) and also buildings and monuments that, quite apart from their utility, enhanced their towns architecturally (temples, porticoes, theaters, gymnasia, fortifications . . .). Sanctuaries too would sometimes either fully or partially fund construction or restoration of sacred buildings or monuments. In the Hellenistic period, in subject cities, kings would sometimes foot the bills for the construction of public edifices such as porticoes, from which they would then derive revenues in the form of rents and taxes. Architectural constructions, both civic and religious, cost huge sums, as we know from accounts, contracts, estimates, and reports engraved in stone. Some of the best-preserved documents relate to the construction of the Athenian acropolis in the second half of the fifth century B.C. (the Parthenon and the Erechtheion in particular), the construction of Philo's arsenal in Piraeus in 347/6, the refurbishment of the sanctuary at Epidaurus between roughly 370 and 250, the construction of the Temple of Zeus at Lebadea in the Hellenistic period, and that of the Temple of Apollo at Didyma whose accounts provide information dating from the mid-third century right down to the end of the second century B.C. These texts reveal a number of constants.

Costs obviously varied according to the scale of the work undertaken and the price of labor, materials, and transport. In some cases these were considerable. The cost of the Parthenon, for example, has been estimated at 470 talents, that is to say 2,820,000 drachmas or more, and that of the sanctuary at Epidaurus at between 240 and 290 talents. Rather than multiply examples, it will perhaps be more helpful to draw attention to the cities' financial capacities. Of course, some projects were ill-considered and ruinous and were never completed, like the Didyma project; others required the efforts of several generations and numerous benefactors. Yet others had to be undertaken as a matter of urgency or in poor conditions, in view of imminent warfare or after an earthquake. Cities sometimes resorted to forced labor. For instance, Agrigentum and other Sicilian towns used prisoners taken at the battle of Himera (in 480 B.C.) to bring many works to completion (Diodorus Siculus, XI.25). Around 400 B.C., Dionysius of Syracuse rapidly fortified the Epipolae, a vast plateau to the west of the town, by bringing in from the countryside around 60,000 freemen and 6,000 teams of oxen (Diodorus Siculus, XIV.18). At Didyma, the sanctuary provided the labor of its own sacred slaves (*hieroi paides*), paying for the cost of their upkeep and equipment.

But cities were not always caught at a disadvantage or with inadequate funds. Sometimes they had large financial surpluses at their disposal, as Athens did when it tapped the booty offered to Athena at the time of the Persian Wars in order to restore its acropolis. Miletus, for its part, funded the construction work at Didyma over a long period. Cities would often appeal to the generosity of the entire population, urging them to make contributions to supplement the city's other resources. As many texts show, overall they managed to draw on a variety of means: public and sacred funds, private contributions, loans, gifts from benefactors, and so on. Many of these public works were not of an urgent nature, so their cost could be spread over considerable periods of time. The construction of the sanctuary at Epidaurus, for example, took around one hundred twenty years, and many constructions at Delos, the Temple of Apollo and the theater in particular, took the better part of the third century. The constructions themselves were built to last for many generations.

Major building sites generally involved many different types of workers. Gangs of conscripted laborers might make up part of the labor force, particularly for the nonskilled tasks; but professionals were always indispensable. Plutarch lists a number of those employed by Athens (*Life of Pericles* 12.6: Austin and Vidal-Naquet, no. 90): carpenters, sculptors, blacksmiths, stonecutters, gilders, ivory workers, painters, inlayers, chiselers . . . Such specialists, freemen for the most part, formed teams under the direction of citizens or metics, many of which would move from one city to another or even as far afield as Persia, wherever their services were in demand. Such mobility indicates that their skills were rare: certain projects, those at Epidaurus for example, seem to have been suspended precisely for lack of an adequate labor force. The accounts concerning the Erechtheion in Athens reveal that citizens, metics, and slaves all worked side by side and received the same wage for the same work, either per day or per task, although a slave would no doubt be obliged to hand over at least part of his pay to his master. Some wages may have been paid directly by the city, but the usual practice was to divide up the work, invite tenders for it, and then distribute it among a number of entrepreneurs. Other inscriptions have preserved comparable examples. On Delos, the accounts of the *hieropoioi* of the period of independence, or at least those of the first half of the third century, which are better preserved, testify to considerable variations in wages and also show that Delian citizens probably outnumbered slaves. All these examples relate to public works, that is to say to projects that were notable for their size, their common use, and the number of specialists employed, so that we cannot draw from them any conclusions about wages in the private sector.

Warfare and Defense

Should warfare, which played an important role in the life of the cities, also be described, in all seriousness, as an example of public enterprise? As we have seen (p. 27), it could certainly generate huge profits. The protection and defense of towns and territories, preparations for conflicts, and warfare in the full sense of the term, once it broke out, also meant heavy expenditure, however, above all for powerful and ambitious cities. Much of that money was invested in permanent constructions (ramparts, fortifications in the countryside, gymnasia, ship sheds, arsenals, and so on), whose completion was generally entrusted to private individuals (as we have seen above). Other expenses provided for training, equipment, pay, and provisions and support for ephebes, guards, and troops. It is true that every hoplite (heavy infantryman) provided his own basic equipment, and, in general, his weaponry would be made in private workshops. But the cities themselves provided some items. In the fourth century

B.C., for example, Athens not only paid the wages of the ten *sōphronistai* (disciplinary officers in charge of the ephebes) and probably also those of the *paidotribai* (physical trainers responsible for *paides* or adolescents) and the masters of arms, but it also allotted four obols per day to every ephebe and provided the shields and spears of their second-year contingent (Aristotle, *The Athenian Constitution* 42). Exceptional orders were sometimes also made. Thus, in 399 Dionysius of Syracuse summoned numerous workers (*technitai*) from Sicily, Italy, and Greece to make weapons and projectiles, in preparation for war against the Carthaginians (Diodorus Siculus, XIV.41).

Fleets of warships generated the heaviest expenses of all. At different periods a number of cities nurtured maritime ambitions: Athens, Samos, Mytilene, Chios, Rhodes, Corinth, Corcyra, Syracuse, and Marseilles, for instance. These used their own funds to construct and maintain warships, presupposing the existence of shipyards, docks, ship sheds, and arsenals. The program of Dionysius of Syracuse mentioned above, quite apart from the refurbishing of one hundred ten (or one hundred fifty) ships, also allowed for the construction of over two hundred new warships and one hundred sixty ship sheds (Diodorus Siculus, XIV.42). After the 227 earthquake (Polybius, V.88–89), the gifts that kings and tyrants presented to Rhodes included, among other items, ten fully equipped penteremes (ships with five levels of oarsmen), enough grain for the crews of ten triremes, beams of split pine sufficient for the construction of ten penteremes and ten triremes, sailcloth, and various other products (wood, tow, pitch, resin, and horsehair) destined for the construction and equipment of the ships. Polybius (V.88.1) also mentions the city's dockyards (*neōria*), and Strabo (XIV.2.5) refers to its *naustathma,* that is to say the harbor's anchorage, its docks, its ship sheds, and its depots. Strabo also briefly describes an ancestral custom obliging wealthy Rhodians, probably ever since the beginning of the Hellenistic period, to fund the living expenses (*diatrophē*) of humble folk (*penētes*) so that "the city should not lack whatever was necessary (*chreia*), in particular for naval expeditions (*naustoliai*)." Despite the obscurity of certain details, it seems clear that the city, not content to invite tenders for construction work, for the upkeep of the fleet, and to pay the workers' wages, regularly obliged those workers to join teams of forced labor paid for by contributions from its wealthy citizens.

No city, however, made such great and durable efforts as Athens did in the classical period. In the fifth century it maintained a fleet of, on average, three hundred triremes. Following an unproductive period lasting about a quarter of a century, shipbuilding picked up again, peaking in 330–325, when it produced over four hundred vessels, most of which were triremes. We possess a few figures relating to this subject. The construction of ship sheds in the fifth century, in Piraeus, cost 1,000 talents, an enormous sum (6 million drachmas). At the end of the Peloponnesian War they were demolished, only to be rebuilt fifty years later, and in 330–325, according to naval inventories, 372 slipways (*neōsoikoi*) were built or renovated. The cost of the triremes (the construction of a ship and repairs to it, the wages of the crew and their provisions) was shared by the city and the wealthiest citizens, who took it in turns to fund the rigging and command of one ship for one year. (This, known as a trierarchy, was the most onerous of all liturgies.) Between 480 and 325, Athens poured huge sums into such projects, but it is not possible to estimate them with any degree of accuracy. It is possible, though, to estimate the cost of every fourth-century trierarchy at 3,000 drachmas per year on average, or even twice that amount during warfare, when extensive repairs might prove necessary.

The shipyards depended upon the services of many teams of skilled workers (joiners, carpenters, makers of rope and sails, painters, among others) and labor forces composed of both free-men and slaves. But we possess very little information about them. Probably, as in the construction of buildings, the work was divided between a number of teams, and tenders were accepted from entrepreneurs advised by architects. These teams of skilled workers, too, were no doubt mobile, for their skills qualified them for all kinds of jobs.

In the world of craft industries as in that of agriculture, we thus find many different types of activity. Small workshops were no doubt rather vulnerable, since they were dependent upon both the fluctuating availability of raw materials and also upon the level of demand for their finished products. Larger businesses, thanks to their size and their diversity, were certainly more stable and more profitable. The proportion of smaller to larger businesses obviously varied from one city to another and one period to another, but in the Hellenistic and Roman periods larger businesses certainly multiplied. Like political developments, they indicate the increasing domination of wealthy minorities adept at investing in public projects. We shall be returning to these patterns of behavior. (See pp. 138–43.)

Public enterprises had important economic consequences for both cities and individuals; they created not only employment but also a labor market, at least from time to time. On this subject, Plutarch is often cited. According to him, the work on the

Athenian acropolis brought well-being or abundance (*euporia*) to the city's entire population (*Life of Pericles* 12.6: Austin and Vidal-Naquet, no. 90). That result is undeniable, as the citizens of Athens, like those of other cities, were well aware. But such projects constituted above all pursuit of political and religious objectives and considerations of prestige. Similarly, exploitation of gold and silver mines certainly aimed to enrich a city, but that wealth was consequential mainly from a political perspective. From this point of view, the Rhodian institution described above (p. 112) is particularly interesting, for it was permanent. Strabo comments that in this way the Rhodians took care of the humbler members of their society, seeking thereby to win their support (*synechein*). A few lines earlier, he had praised the concern for good order (*eunomia*) that characterized this city. The methods it adopted were original, but they were inspired first and foremost by a desire to avoid social tensions and preserve harmony among the citizens.

PRIMARY TEXTS
The Development of the World of Craftsmanship

In small towns the same workman makes chairs and doors and ploughs and tables, and often this same artisan builds houses, and even so he is thankful if he can only find employment enough to support him. And it is, of course, impossible for a man of many trades to be proficient in all of them. In large cities, on the other hand, inasmuch as many people have demands to make upon each branch of industry, one trade alone, and very often even less than a whole trade, is enough to support a man: one man, for instance, makes shoes for men, and another for women; and there are places even where one man earns a living by only stitching shoes, another by cutting them out, another by sewing the uppers together, while there is another who performs none of these operations but only assembles the parts. It follows therefore, as a matter of course, that he who devotes himself to a very highly specialized line of work is bound to do it in the best possible manner.

Xenophon, *Cyropaedia* VIII.2.5, translated by
Walter Miller, The Loeb Classical Library, 1914

The Laurion Silver Mines of Attica
in the Mid-fourth Century B.C.

As for the silver mines, I believe that if a proper system of working were introduced, a vast amount of money would be obtained from them apart from our other sources of revenue. I want to point out the possibilities of these mines to those who do not know. For once you realize their possibilities, you will be in a better position to consider how the mines should be managed.

Now, we all agree that the mines have been worked for many generations. At any rate, no one even attempts to date the beginning of mining operations. And yet, although digging and the removal of silver ore have been carried on for so long a time, note how small is the size of the dumps compared with the virgin and silver-laden hills. And it is continually being found that, so far from shrinking, the silver-yielding area extends further and further.

Well, so long as the maximum number of workmen was employed in them, no one ever wanted for a job; in fact, there were always more jobs than the labourers could deal with. And even at the present day no owner of slaves employed in the mines reduces the number of his men; on the contrary, every master obtains as many more as he can. The fact is, I imagine, that when there are few diggers and searchers, the amount of metal recovered is small, and when there are many, the total of ore discovered is multiplied. Hence of all the industries with which I am acquainted this is the only one in which expansion of business excites no jealousy.

Xenophon, *Ways and Means* (*Poroi*) IV.1–4, translated by E. C. Marchant, The Loeb Classical Library, 1968

FOUR

Trade

Over the centuries trade made great progress within cities and, above all, between them. Of course development was neither regular nor uniform, and it took place alongside the expansion of agriculture and craft industries. But it was the development of what was truly commerce, effected by the use of money, that fueled change and most clearly distinguished between some cities and others. It is not possible to estimate the volume of trade in the Greek economy. The number of professional traders was certainly far lower than that of people engaged in agriculture. Peasants, however, and craftsmen in particular, acted as salesmen for their own products, so that, in one way or another, trade involved many people. Trading transactions left their mark upon many literary, epigraphical, and archaeological sources, in a very uneven fashion, of course, depending on sectors and regions, but sometimes in such a way as to shed light on the details of certain activities. So much will become clear from the diversity of the problems tackled below, even if they are presented in a general fashion. A study of them raises a number of fundamental questions that have been at the heart of numerous debates.

TRADING CONDITIONS
Constraints

Throughout antiquity, the development of trade was to a certain extent restricted by such impediments as the multiplicity of frontiers, the risks of warfare, piracy, banditry, and plunder (pp. 24–27 and 36–37), and also by the efforts to achieve self-sufficiency persistent in the agriculture and craft-industry sectors. (See above, pp. 85–86 and 93–95.) Besides, trade always has depended upon demand, just like the products of craftsmen. In the ancient Greek world, information took time to circulate, especially over great distances, and was in general a matter of personal contacts. Finally, despite all the progress achieved over the centuries, the slow pace of transport always handicapped the movement of both people and merchandise and added greatly to the costs of commercial transactions.

Overland transport, using beasts of burden or wagons, was generally limited to local trading over short distances, to transfer agricultural products from the fields to the granaries and cellars and from there to the marketplaces, for example, or to convey craft products, blocks of stone from quarries or wood felled in the forests, to local towns or ports. Beasts of burden and wagons could cover little more than fifteen or twenty kilometers a day. Many roads were no more than tracks, hard to negotiate in bad weather but viable (and more appropriate) for beasts of burden. For carts, some networks of paved roads existed, with relay posts along the way, at least in the more developed regions and those that made the most of the efforts of the Persian kings and the Hellenistic sovereigns. To these the Romans later added long, solidly constructed roads. Of course, their purpose was initially strategic (they were used for the conveyance of correspondence and the movements of troops, magistrates, and diplomats), but they also facilitated trade. Since they were much used and were patrolled, they offered more security against banditry.

Few rivers were navigable, but merchants took to the sea whenever they could. Transport ships, which the Greeks described as round, to distinguish them from their narrow triremes, navigated mostly with sails. They were thus dependent on the winds, which were often capricious. From spring to autumn, navigation was relatively safe, despite the violence of the winds from the north that blew in the Aegean during the summer. In winter it was interrupted or slowed by the shortness of daylight, bad weather, squalls, and storms. Certain currents and reefs had to be avoided. But as generation after generation gathered more experience, routes became familiar, described in many works (known as *periploi*) and sometimes indicated on maps and books of seaports. Travel by sea was usually undertaken by daylight, when one could see or calculate one's position, but sometimes ships sailed at night and steered by the stars. Rather than sail over open water, ancient navigators preferred coasting, with ships putting in at a series of ports where merchandise was bought and sold on a daily basis. The larger ports were equipped with depots that stored goods from many different places, which could be redistributed from there. The capacity of transport vessels varied, but over the centuries it increased. To judge by the wrecks that have been found, in the classical period most ships could carry between twenty and seventy tons of cargo. By the Hellenistic period, the average cargo capacity of many ships was one hundred twenty tons or more, and it continued to increase. The time sea voyages took varied greatly depending on the season, navigating conditions, and the number of times a ship put into port. If one reckons the average speed of ships in the classical period to have been around three or four knots, they would cover barely forty kilometers in one day. Deep-sea navigation progressed during the Hellenistic period, at least on certain routes, as from Alexandria to Rome. But coasting remained the general rule.

The Diffusion of Minted Coins and the Monetarization of the Economy

As we have seen (above, pp. 55–57), trade benefited greatly from the introduction of minted money. Of course the use of money did not spread everywhere at the same rate, but it was certainly the Greeks who, quite rapidly, set up the first monetary system in history and employed it as a universal means of evaluation and payment. They used silver above all, the precious metal most readily available, and they tended to hoard gold when they had any. Coins of both metals could thus serve either as reserves or as merchandise. Gold was obviously the more precious. Its relation to silver remained more or less constant at one to thirteen and one-third in the Persian kingdom. Then, in fifth-century Greece, it rose to its maximum value. In Athens, in 434/3, gold was worth sixteen and two-thirds times as much as silver. In the years that followed, that ratio fell to one to fifteen, as it also did in southern Italy and Sicily. By the end of the century it stood at around one to fourteen or one to twelve. In the early fourth century, that was the ratio obtaining in a number of cities, and in 335, in Athens, the ratio was one to ten. Eventually that ratio of one to ten remained the rule throughout the Hellenistic period in the zone where the Attic standard was recognized. That progressive devaluation of gold resulted from supply and demand and from the relative abundance or scarcity of both metals. As for bronze, a low-grade metal, its value was primarily fiduciary, and it was limited to local use. The value of a *chalkous,* a bronze coin, was, depending on the local system, either one-eighth or one-twelfth of an obol.

Although silver coins were increasingly used in the fifth century, in the fourth century, small bronze ones, specifically intended for local use and day-to-day transactions, began to be systematically minted. No doubt payments and dues continued to be made in kind. As late as the Hellenistic period, for example, agricultural taxes were paid in the form of a proportion of the harvests, produce that the tax farmers and collectors then had to sell on in order to hand over proper money to the cities (or kings) that employed them. Some goods could also be exchanged, following a monetary evaluation, without actually resorting to the use of metal money. By this time the monetarization of the entire economy was already under way. Quite apart from making trading more flexible, minted coins made it possible for individuals to acquire movable fortunes that were, as the Greeks put it, "invisible," and minted coins also promoted the development of credit.

The Primitivist school of thought has often emphasized the scarcity of coins in circulation, a factor liable to slow down economic development; and the sources do indeed testify to instances of a dearth of coins among both cities and individuals. However, apart from exceptional times, such as those of warfare, which could delay the arrival of precious metals, those shortages were for the most part only temporary, doubtless provoked by hoarding. This took two forms: private (archaeological excavations have revealed many hoards of treasure dating from all periods) and also public (accounts have survived, often referring to monetary reserves kept in sanctuaries, some of considerable size). Gold and silver always preserved their value as metals. The tendency nowadays is to upgrade the productivity of mints that marked coins with an imprint. During the last two centuries B.C. and the following two, the volume of coins in circulation was comparable to that available in seventeenth-century Holland or eighteenth-century France.

The Greeks understood how monetary circulation functioned. In the *Poroi* (IV.10), for example, Xenophon refers to the law of supply and demand in connection with the devaluation of gold and the stability of silver. But it is unlikely that citizens were particularly concerned to maintain the circulation of a sufficient quantity of coins, or even to control the volume in their own territories so as to affect prices. At any rate, no documents exist to support such hypotheses.

Monetary Unifications

The fact that each city minted its own coins and in many cases insisted that they be used in its own territory made for wide diversity and many occasions when it was necessary to change currencies. Fortunately, the weight of the basic unit, a stater or a drachma, varied between only a few systems, for many cities

used a common standard weight. The most ancient and originally the most widely dispersed was the Aegina standard,
according to which a stater weighed roughly 12.2 grams. This
was adopted throughout much of mainland Greece (the
Peloponnese, Boeotia, Phocis, Thessaly), in Crete, most of the
Cyclades, Caria, Teos, Miletus, and the colonies that Miletus
established around the Black Sea. The standard recognized in
Attica and Euboea, with one drachma weighing 4.3 grams, was
to prove very successful. Certain currencies soon won the pref-
erence of traders and thus acquired an international role. The
ones most widely used in the classical period were the gold
Persian daric (which weighed about 8.4 grams), the electrum
stater of Cyzicus (about 16.4 grams), and the silver Attic
tetradrachma (about 17.2 grams).

In the early fifth century, however, the Athenian currency
progressively took over the Aegean world and even lands
beyond, partly for its excellent alloy and its abundance due to
the Laurion mines (see above, p. 104), but also as a result of the
political domination of the Delian League, founded in 478/7 B.C.
A number of cities now gradually abandoned the minting of
their own silver coins and adopted the "little owls" of Athens for
their external trading, continuing meanwhile to issue bronze
coins for internal use. This gradual supremacy received official
confirmation just before or during the Peloponnesian War (the
date is controversial), when Athens imposed its own currency,
weights, and measures upon its allies (Austin and Vidal-
Naquet, no. 101). The impact of that decision is debatable, and
a number of cities did continue to mint their own silver coins.
But it presented a practical advantage for the Athenians, for it
unified the coinage in which allied cities paid their tribute,

and thereby simplified the calculations of the Athenian administration. Furthermore, it constituted an expression of
Athenian authority and power, diminishing the autonomy of
its allies. And finally, it presented Athens with a tangible
advantage, for now the allies' tribute payments had to be made
with Athenian tetradrachmas, whose quality was indisputable
and whose production increased. The international status of
Athenian money was thus further enhanced. Even the reverses
that Athens suffered in the Peloponnesian War, followed by
defeat in 404 and ensuing difficulties, affected that Athenian
supremacy for no more than a few years, for it was rapidly
reestablished. In the mid-fourth century, Xenophon referred
to it explicitly in a passage in his *Poroi* (III.2). It was maintained right down to the beginning of the Hellenistic period,
despite the appearance, in the mid-fourth century (this date,
too, is controversial), of Philip II of Macedon's gold staters
(which weighed 8.6 grams). There was a clear distinction, as
Plato notes (*Laws* V, 742a), between currencies in common circulation and those limited to local daily use. The minting of
local bronze coins intensified in the fourth century and became
general practice thereafter.

Following his conquests, Alexander extended the phenomenon of minted money by swiftly introducing large numbers of
silver coins based on the Attic standard and bearing his effigy.
These "Alexanders" were produced by kings and cities in
numerous regions, using their own mints, and thus became the
international currency of the Seleucid East and most of the eastern Mediterranean throughout the Hellenistic period. The most
notable exception was Egypt, where the Lagid sovereigns created
a closed area using much lighter coins. Other currencies that

became international at different periods were those of Rhodes, the Achaean League, and Pergamum. Meanwhile, though, local issues of bronze and silver coins persisted, for internal use.

With the Roman conquest, the unification process was completed. From the second century B.C. onward, the denarius was introduced into the eastern Mediterranean by the Roman legions. It did not begin to circulate widely until the mid-first century and at first served simply as money of account, while the coins in circulation continued to be "Alexanders" or local currencies. However, a denarius was recognized to be worth as much as a drachma of Attic weight. Eventually, from the time of Augustus onward, some kind of unity was established as imperial coins of gold, silver, and bronze were regularly minted and diffused. The minting of coins was the prerogative of the emperor, though it might take place elsewhere than in Rome. Traditional currencies were nevertheless still abundant and remained in circulation. Their denominations and standards continued to be used alongside imperial money for provincial issues of coins minted under the Roman administration, and for local issues, mainly of bronze coins. Exchange facilities thus continued to be needed. But what was new, as in the Hellenistic period, was the circulation of an international currency. No central authority had either the ambition or the means to impose the use of a single currency everywhere.

The Advent and Diffusion of Banks

As early as the second half of the sixth century B.C., in commercial centers, the need to change money created the profession of moneychanger. The following century saw the appearance of proper banks, when moneychangers began to accept deposits and to work with them. At that time banks were known as *trapezai* (as indeed they are in modern Greek), so called after the "tables" (or counters) used in banking operations. Bankers themselves were called *trapezitai.* In the cities, the profession expanded from the classical period onward, enabling at least some individuals to acquire large fortunes. The most famous of them was Pasio. He began as a slave owned by a couple of Athenian bankers but was given his freedom. At the beginning of the fourth century he took over the bank of his two erstwhile masters and was eventually awarded citizenship in recognition of his services to the city. At his death, he left a real-estate fortune worth 20 talents (120,000 drachmas) and credits worth over 50 talents (300,000 drachmas), plus his bank situated in Piraeus, which brought in 10,000 drachmas, and a workshop producing shields that was worth 6,000 (Demosthenes, *For Phormio* 5 and 11).

Banks would accept deposits from private individuals who wished to leave their funds somewhere safe, either to use for making payments or transfers (using an order made out to the banker, not to the beneficiary), or else to generate interest. In the cities the interest rate was seldom addressed by any laws or regulations. Yet, except in extreme conditions, it remained stable for centuries. In the fourth century it was normally 12 percent; then in the Hellenistic period it dropped to 10 percent, partly as a result of Alexander's large injection of money. Bankers would also provide certain services, such as the drawing up and storing of contracts. What mattered most was, of course, credit. Banks would generally offer short-term loans with no fixed deadline and at quite high interest rates (18 percent or more). But their clients, whether seeking loans or wishing to deposit money, were as a rule men of wealth or at least ample means. Most humble folk would have no funds to deposit and would borrow money, if they had to, from friends, family, or moneylenders. The motives of wealthy borrowers have been the subject of much debate. Athenian sources suggest that most of them simply needed extra liquid funds momentarily, to provide a daughter with a dowry or to fulfill civic obligations such as liturgies, for example. These were—as the phrase has it—consumer loans. In some cases, such funds may have been invested in business ventures. But, as we shall see (below, pp. 139–40), in this domain the riskiest loans were not advanced by the banks. Our sources contain no trace of bank loans made to cities.

Most banks were privately owned, although public banks (*dēmosiai trapezai*) made an appearance in the Hellenistic period in cities such as Athens, Delos, Tenos, Cos, Miletus, and others. Some of these would grant loans to private individuals, but most played a purely technical role in the administration of cities, carrying out routine operations such as guarding public funds, managing certain budgetary tasks, collecting taxes, paying expenses, advancing funds to accounts that were momentarily depleted, and so forth. In similar fashion, certain rich sanctuaries, the best-known of which was Delos, performed some banking operations (see above, p. 48) at interest rates that were lower than those of private banks or private individuals.

DIFFERENT LEVELS OF TRADING

We should distinguish between several levels of trading, even though they were in fact closely interconnected.

Local Trading

After the Bronze Age, cities and their subdivisions constituted the natural and, as it were, immutable frameworks for local trading throughout antiquity. This was certainly the most ancient type of trading, and it remained the most stable, whatever the political changes. It was probably at this humble level that ancient trading played its greatest role, day in, day out, not—to be sure—by reason of the value of the products traded or the size of the sums of money in play, but rather because of the number of transactions and people involved. For centuries, local inhabitants continued to trade surpluses produced by their crops, stock-raising, fishing, and other connected activities such as forestry and gathering plants, as well as products of skilled craftsmanship. Gradually certain cultivators steered either all or some of their produce in the direction of the local market, a move that already presupposed relatively diversified trading and a regular use of money. Thus, around the mid-fifth century B.C., Pericles was systematically selling all his crops in the market. (See above, p. 86.) One century later (around 330), likewise in Attica, the wealthy landowner Phaenippus, whose estate covered an area of between forty and sixty hectares, sold wood he had felled, transporting it to buyers throughout the year by means of six donkeys; from this he made over twelve drachmas a day (Pseudo-Demosthenes, *Against Phaenippus* 7 and 24). All such practices reflected a desire for self-sufficiency at the level of the city itself.

It was within this context that shopkeepers or retailers (*kapēloi*) made their appearance, as early as the archaic period. These acted simply as intermediaries, for not all agricultural and craft products were sold directly by their producers.

Furthermore, produce and objects brought in from outside, which soon came to supplement local products, also ended up in the marketplace, where all retailing activities took place.

Initially, trading activities were no doubt fairly unregimented. But in the interests of convenience and, above all, taxation, in urban areas certain particular places came to be set aside for them. They were located in urban centers, generally in the public space of the agora (from the verb *ageirein*), which was also used for political or religious gatherings. In some cities, however (Thessaly, for example), the commercial market was separate from the so-called free agora, where no trading took place. In the eyes of Aristotle, this was the ideal situation (*Politics* 1331a30–b4): Austin and Vidal-Naquet, no. 129). As cities took shape, markets were made progressively more convenient, and soon, from the sixth century on, once the great public and sacred constructions were completed, they were equipped with proper buildings. In the classical period and thereafter, trading and the facilities for it gradually took over more and more space in city agoras. Cities of a certain size might even accommodate more than one urban agora (as in Athens and Piraeus) as well as local ones. (In Attica these would serve individual demes.) Each agora could be divided, on different days, between markets for cheeses, animals, grain, meat, fish, and so on, as opposed to being a general market (*agora pantopōlis*).

Popular Festivals (Panēgyreis)

Trading was also associated with the festivals that cities celebrated. Over and above the religious ceremonies and the athletic and musical competitions such festivals normally featured, cities sometimes seized the opportunity to lay on a special market, not just to provide for the needs of the participants, but also to promote trading of many kinds. There were many such festivals, and they generally lasted for several days. Some were annual, others were held several times a year, yet others only every three or five years. Most were local or regional; others were pan-Hellenic, and these multiplied as the years passed, particularly from the second half of the third century B.C. They attracted crowds, sometimes huge ones, of pilgrims, artists, athletes, and the simply curious. Their profane (nonsacred) element was comparable to that of the fairs of the Middle Ages. These gatherings were known as *panēgyreis,* a term that usually covered the festival as a whole but in some cases applied above all to its commercial side. But often enough the latter was simply known as the agora.

Whether small or large-scale, these fairs did not last for long and frequently took place on temporary sites with temporary stalls. But they were held regularly, and they supplemented ordinary day-to-day trading. From this point of view, they occupied an intermediary position between local and regional trading. On the one hand, by gathering together an exceptional collection of people, they gave local cultivators, craftsmen, and merchants a chance to sell their products. On the other, they attracted local and itinerant merchants who brought along and sold, possibly more cheaply than usual, products that local people could not find on a day-to-day basis. This, at any rate, is the kind of picture evoked by Pausanias (X.32.14–16) in his description of the festival celebrated in honor of Isis by the small city of Tithorea, in Phocis, twice a year, in spring and autumn. The festival lasted three days. The merchants constructed their own shops or sheds (*skēnai*) out of reeds and planks. The fair was open only on the third day. It sold slaves, animals, clothing, silver, and gold. It closed down quite early in the day, as the afternoon was devoted to sacrifices.

Regional and Long-distance Trading

It would be hard not to present these two levels of trade in combination, for they shared much in common. Rather than lump them together right from the start, as often happens, however, in the wake of a number of recent studies it is worth stressing the importance of regional trading, whose volume was always greater than or at least equivalent to that of long-distance trading. The fact is that, given the slowness and cost of transport, most products at all times circulated over the shortest possible distances. It was, in short, a matter of close relations between neighboring cities linked by common traditions, complementary interests, and adequate means of communication. Such trading included non-Greek peoples of the hinterland as well as the Aegean world. Many of these networks appear to have extended for no more than a few dozen kilometers, but they were naturally flexible, and there were many of them.

From the eighth century onward, following a decline in the previous period, trading recovered on a wider scale and even involved the entire Mediterranean area. Greek trading relations expanded greatly in the course of the period of colonization, in parallel with those of the Phoenicians and the Etruscans. From coastal cities, contacts reached out into more distant regions: Gaul, Spain, Central Europe, North Africa, and the Near East. The most active cities, both at this time and later, were also positioned at the hub of regional networks: in Asia Minor, these were Miletus, Smyrna, Phocaea, and Phaselis; in mainland Greece, Aegina (before the competition and domination of Athens), Athens (from the sixth century on), Corinth (thanks to its position on the isthmus between the east and the west; in the Ionian Sea, Corinth's colony Corcyra (for a similar reason); in the Aegean Sea, Thasos; in the Straits, Cyzicus and Byzantium (through which many trade routes passed); in the Nile Delta, Naucratis (initially just a trading post where grain bound for the Greek world would be brought); in Africa, Cyrene; in the West, Tarentum, Syracuse, and Marseilles. Stable networks were also established between metropolises and their colonies, for example between Miletus and the Black Sea, and between Corinth and Sicily. In the classical period, thanks to the political power of Athens, Piraeus was for two centuries the major transit and redistribution center for the whole of the eastern Mediterranean. Many authors have marveled at the wide variety of products that were to be found there (Austin and Vidal-Naquet, nos. 83 and 85). Athens at this time headed a powerful alliance. Its resources and wealth far outstripped those of other cities. Its fleet of warships was in a position to police the seas and provide escorts for convoys of merchandise, those from the Black Sea heading for Piraeus with cargoes of grain in particular.

In the Hellenistic period, Egypt and much of the Near East opened up to new contacts, some of which stretched as far afield as black Africa, Arabia, India, and the Far East. In the eastern Mediterranean, the great commercial axes now shifted. Rhodes, which took over from Athens in the Aegean Sea, and Alexandria, the Lagid capital, were the two most important intersections between the east and the west and between the north and the south. From 166 on, the free port of Delos, which Rome created, became a center of commerce and business in its turn. We know that the political events of the Hellenistic period adversely affected production and trade in the eastern Mediterranean, to the point of ruining a number of cities for a long time. (See above, p. 24.) However, the advent of the Roman Empire with its *pax Romana* helped to speed the recovery and expansion of trade. While Rome siphoned off more and more products and slaves, and became the major financial and commercial center in the Mediterranean, other cities on the Greek mainland acquired or recovered a certain importance. One was Corinth, destroyed by Rome in 146 and refounded one hundred years later, which became the capital of the province of Achaea. Others included Nicopolis (founded by Augustus) Patras, Athens, Argos, and Philippi. The list ought also to include many other cities, such as Nicomedia and Ephesus in Asia Minor, for a large number of cities were now trading over more or less great distances.

The circulating products were, with a few variants, the same at both local and long-distance levels, and they are relatively well known to us. Many responded to basic needs: grain, wine, oil, vegetables, fruits, fish, animal skins, leather, wool, fabrics, clothing, slaves, livestock, wood, stone, marble, metals, tools, weaponry, ceramic objects, and so on. Obviously enough, perishable foodstuffs could not survive long voyages unless they could be dried, as fruits were, or preserved in salt, like fish (which could likewise be dried or pickled). By reason of their size and weight, heavy materials such as blocks of stone and rough wood could be transported by sea only with difficulty, unless they were divided into lighter pieces. Certain items, such as grain, metals, wood for building, and slaves too, could often be found only in distant regions. As for luxury products such as jewels, costly clothing, works of art, ivory, perfumes, and spices, it was perfectly possible to transport these over long distances, as their light weight and high prices offset the cost of transport and its attendant risks. But the infinite variety of these trading transactions defies description within these limited pages. Readers should consult the examples of local products listed above, in chapters 2 and 3 (pp. 87–88 and 98–99).

Grain (*sitos*) was a vital foodstuff that many cities had to import on a regular basis, sometimes from distant lands, in particular from the Black Sea region, Cyrenaïca, Egypt, and Sicily. This was a problem addressed by many literary and epigraphical sources, above all by the Attic orators, where Athens was concerned. According to Demosthenes (*Against Leptines* 31–32, dated 355/4 B.C.: Austin and Vidal-Naquet, no. 81), no other city was obliged to import as much grain as Athens, and half of it (400,000 *medimnoi*) came from the kingdom of the Cimmerian Bosporus (in the Straits of Kertch, to the north of the Black Sea. (See below, p. 157.) That impressive figure has prompted many estimates of the city's needs, the size of its population, its average consumption, and its own production capacity. But the fact is that no one knows whether it represented an annual average or simply the quantity imported in one particular year of good or bad harvests. We do know, thanks to a recently published law passed in 374/3, that at this time Athens collected a tax in kind on the grain harvested on the islands of Lemnos, Imbros, and Scyros, where a number of Athenians had established themselves (Rhodes & Osborne, no. 96). The annual total of this tax has been calculated at over 31,000 *medimnoi,* four-fifths of which were barley, one-fifth wheat.

One clause in this law established the relation between one *me-dimnos,* a measure of volume, and one talent, a measure of weight. This led to the discovery that these grains were lighter than had been thought: one *medimnos* of wheat was the equivalent of roughly thirty-one kilos, not forty or more. In other words, if the grain from the Black Sea was of comparable weight, 400,000 *medimnoi* was the equivalent of about 12,400 tons of wheat or 10,800 tons of barley. As for imports from the islands of wheat and barley together, they came annually to close on 1,000 tons. We also know that between 330 and 325, a time of considerable food shortages, Cyrene exported more than 800,000 *medimnoi* of grain (*sitos*). Several of the totals relating to deliveries have disappeared from the inscription that lists them, but it is clear that Athens alone received 100,000 *medimnoi,* while Argos, for example, took delivery of half that amount, and Delphi ten times less. The equivalent weight in kilos cannot be established with certainty, since it is not known whether these were Laconian or Aeginetan *medimnoi* (Rhodes & Osborne, no. 96).

These products circulated mainly by sea, and they had to pass through embarkation and disembarkation points known as *emporia* before being sent on to the *agorai* to be sold by retailers. There were various types of *emporia,* but the point to remember is what characterized them within the framework of the cities: the *emporion* was the place where all imported and exported goods were traded and inspected. Given that most cities had a seaport, or even two (Corinth) or three (Athens), the *emporion* was frequently part of a port. It was always strictly delimited. In the early archaic period, port facilities were relatively rudimentary, but little by little the cities improved them, as they did their agoras, and provided them with all the necessary buildings and equipment: piers, lighthouses, wharves, sheds, depots, customs houses in which to declare the merchandise, and others for the payment of taxes, and so forth.

Today it is no longer thought, as the Modernists believed, that there was one, single, vast market serving the whole Mediterranean or even the entire ancient world, a market in which all kinds of products were transported over long distances and then traded. It is true that from the archaic period onward long trading routes became established and thereafter were constantly diversifying. From the Hellenistic period on, the common Greek language (*Koinē*) was increasingly used in the eastern Mediterranean and the Near East, while under the empire, Latin gradually spread throughout the West. Despite political unification and the pacification of the Mediterranean, however, regional trade remained largely dominant for what are, after all, quite obvious reasons. That was certainly the case in Delos, for example, during its period of independence, that is to say before its *emporion* was declared to be a free port. (See above, p. 133.) Essentially, it traded with the neighboring Cyclades islands, and its prices fluctuated according to local or regional circumstances. Trading in the ancient world was thus divided among many different networks. The merchants themselves probably developed preferences for trading networks with routes and customs they knew and where they maintained relations of hospitality. They would sometimes make the most of price differences and switch from one zone to another in order to profit. So these were by no means closed trading networks. They interacted and also functioned in liaison with the long-distance commerce that was, to some extent, superimposed upon them.

THE BUSINESS WORLD
Types of Merchants

Most men who engaged in business were no doubt unaware that their activities aroused anxiety and provoked censure among certain philosophers. (See above, p. 31.) But we should distinguish between the different types of traders and also between their different social levels, which the Greek language distinguishes clearly enough. It was above all the small-scale shopkeepers of the agora (*kapēloi*) who were reproached for their love of money and their dishonesty. They constituted one of the favorite targets of such comic authors as Aristophanes, and they doubtless commanded scant respect in day-to-day life. But we know very little about them. Many were metics or even slaves who had been set up in shops by their masters. In cities like Athens, however, some of them were citizens.

The *emporion* was the workplace of the *emporoi,* who bought and sold wholesale goods and invested funds in expeditions to more or less distant places. The voyages themselves were the concern of shipowners (*nauklēroi*), who might, of course, also buy, transport, and sell their own merchandise. From the classical period onward, most *emporoi* and *nauklēroi* tended to be metics or visiting foreigners. Their wealth certainly varied enormously. But we know of quite a few *emporoi* thanks to the honorific decrees that various cities voted to thank them for services rendered, such as low-priced sales and gifts of grain in times of hardship. Their generosity, funded by their wealth, earned them the citizens' esteem.

The situation in the archaic period is less clear. Already around 700, Hesiod, in his *Works and Days,* described the kind of maritime trading (*emporië*) that a small-scale cultivator wishing to escape from debt and hunger could practice during the spring and above all in the high summer, to complement his usual work (618–94). At a later date, we know of wealthy aristocrats who engaged in long-distance trade. One was Solon of Athens, who engaged in *emporia*-trading at the end of the seventh century (Plutarch, *Life of Solon* 2). Around the same time, Colaeus of Samos and, in the following century, Sostratus of Aegina were sailing to and fro across the Mediterranean with their companions and their crews (Herodotus IV.152, who describes Colaeus as a *nauklëros*). No doubt these men were selling the surplus produce from their land and buying a variety of goods such as metals and luxury objects, as well as engaging in pillage and piracy. In deals between men of equal rank, trading would probably sometimes take the form of an exchange of prestige gifts, in the manner favored by tyrants or, in the Homeric world, by kings and aristocrats linked by ties of friendship and hospitality (Homer, *Odyssey* 180–89 and 306–18: Austin and Vidal-Naquet, no. 26). So this kind of life was respectable, but it was no doubt not essential to these men, for they were first and foremost landowners and prominent citizens. Professional merchants, some wealthy, some not, also existed, and their numbers were certainly on the increase. But we know very little about them.

The Development of Big Business

It is in classical Athens that we find big business starting up. Of course the desire to grow rich and make profits is as old as the world itself. But this particularly active and prosperous city allowed the tendency more freedom to develop and to spread.

We have already noted a number of indicative signs: the *oikono-mia Attikē* practiced by Pericles and his imitators (p. 87), the science of profit described by Xenophon in his *Oeconomicaus* (pp. 33–34), the headlong rush for money taking place before Aristotle's very eyes (pp. 31–32). But the phenomenon was not peculiar to Athens. If we possessed comparable sources for other cities that were open to commerce, we should certainly detect the same tendencies developing and doing so just as early on. From the Hellenistic period onward in particular, members of high society increasingly went in for these types of investment into agriculture and craft industries. (See above, pp. 87, 98.) And it was thanks to both regional and distant trading outlets that such activities spread more widely. Not only did the men who engaged in them possess vast estates, large herds, and many workshops, but some of them also owned shipping and even private ports or else did business deals with *nauklēroi.* They invested in lucrative ventures, in particular in maritime loans of the kind that we find in fourth-century Athens.

The fitting out of a ship and the purchase of merchandise could require huge investments of capital. Moreover, sea voyages and transport entailed many risks. Hence the introduction of maritime loans. They are relatively well documented, thanks to the speeches of fourth-century Athenian orators, but they probably originated in the previous century. A loan would be advanced to an *emporos* or a *nauklēros* with either his ship or his cargo, or possibly both, as security. The contract covered all eventualities and details: the contents of the cargo, the destination and stopovers in the voyage (either one-way or return), the interest rates and loan securities, the means of recovering the money, and so on. The creditor risked a total loss in the event of a shipwreck, a pirate attack, or other accidents. However, when a voyage was completed successfully, his profit might be as high as 20 or 30 percent. The most ancient example, already extremely detailed, of this type of contract is provided by Ps.-Demosthenes' speech *Against Lacritus* (10–13), which dates from the mid-fourth century (Austin and Vidal-Naquet, no. 121). In this agreement the creditors were an Athenian and a Carystian, while the borrowers were two Phaselitans. We should note that in commerce as in craft industries, partnerships had no legal standing. The law recognized only individuals.

In business deals of this kind, personal relations played a major role, for the granting of huge credits depended upon mutual trust. The men involved knew one another well and worked together to share the costs and risks. They also depended upon such relationships when it came to other financial operations, lending one another sums of money, for example, rather than resorting to a bank. Cities might also prefer to turn to these men when they were in need of loans, as is clear, for example, from six extremely detailed contracts from the island of Amorgos that were engraved in stone at the time of Alexander and his successors (L. Migeotte, *L'emprunt public,* nos. 49–54). A number of these businessmen were certainly metics or foreigners who had grown rich on the proceeds of craft industries and trade. (Indeed, some were themselves *emporoi*.) Lacking real estate, they naturally turned to big business. But some high-society citizens were likewise involved in business, investing their wealth without necessarily acting as the managing directors of their businesses, sometimes even using intermediaries in order to avoid attracting unwelcome attention.

Much has been written about these merchant elites. Clearly, their methods were not those of modern capitalism. Nonetheless, taking into account the skills and means of the period, they responded to an economic rationale, for these were men who understood the value of wealth and also how to use it. So it is not anachronistic to refer to their activities using words such as "capital" and "investment." All the same, when citizens were involved in big business there was a problem, for in most cases they were from families that had produced the city's leading figures from one generation to the next, and, as such, they were expected to lead honorable lives, to be involved in public affairs and be seen to be educated, committed, and generous. Their primary aim was thus not simply to grow rich but to maintain their social rank; and it is clear that many of them were large-scale landowners, in the purest tradition. However, the generosity that was expected of them, their outlay of unproductive expenditure, demanded huge financial assets. That is why they were able to diversify these, as an apposite expression puts it, by doing business without being in business.

Already by the classical period, Athens provides examples of such men. We know of Nicias, who rented out a thousand slaves in the Laurion mines (pp. 105, 106). Although his fame stemmed primarily from his immense fortune (Plutarch, *Life of Nicias* 3.1; 11.2; 15.20), it was his political career that insured that he was classed among the great Athenians of the late fifth century (Aristotle, *The Athenian Constitution* 28.5). We also know that, in the following century, his family owned land in the vicinity of the mines. Even more interesting is the example provided by Demosthenes, although his fortune was much smaller than that of Nicias.

Demosthenes was one of the most eminent statesmen of the fourth century, and he himself recorded the details of his paternal inheritance, which his guardians had mostly squandered before he ever came of age (*Against Aphobus* I.9–11: Austin and Vidal-Naquet, no. 120). The value of that patrimony had been around fourteen talents and included the craft workshops mentioned above (p. 98), together worth 23,000 drachmas; 15,000 drachmas' worth of raw materials (wood, iron, ivory, bronze, dyes); a house worth 3,000 drachmas; furniture, jewelry, clothing, etc., worth 10,000 drachmas; 11,000 drachmas cash; and (a revealing detail) 20,600 drachmas of credit, 7,000 of which had been advanced in the form of maritime loans and 6,000 in loans to friends. Of course, this estimate made by an orator should not be accepted at face value; all the same, it gives us some idea of the size of the sums involved. Curiously, though, there is no mention of real- estate property. It is not known to what extent Demosthenes was able to retrieve his wealth as a result of his lawsuit; but it seems certain that he never did possess land or invest in the mines. He continued to take an interest in large-scale commerce, and his wealth essentially comprised "invisible" assets. However, despite the unorthodox nature of his fortune, he enjoyed great prestige on account of his political activities and his devotion and generosity to his city.

From the late Hellenistic period onward, more and more citizens are to be found among the merchants, entrepreneurs, shipowners, and bankers in large trading cities such as Byzantium, Nicomedia, and Ephesus. Others were meanwhile making their fortunes as orators, sophists, or philosophers, which was more in keeping with the ideal of *scholē*. (See above, p. 29.) Most of these citizens were members of elites, and many of them also held Roman citizenship. The evidence is somewhat vague, however, as the texts do not always record their mercantile activities and most of them seem also to have been landowners. On the other hand, for those who had made their fortunes chiefly as businessmen, access to the circles of city notables was not always easy, despite the prestige enjoyed by certain corporations. For example, the council of Ephesus appears never to have accepted any *naukḷēros* within its ranks.

PUBLIC INTERVENTIONS

As in agriculture and craft industries, most commercial activities remained in the hands of private individuals who engaged in them perfectly freely. But unlike agricultural and craft production, trading took place in a public sector in which divergent interests sometimes surfaced. So it was soon raising problems of order, discipline, and justice as well as concerns about taxation. Furthermore, the world of Greek cities was marked for contention by two constant features: on the one hand, its tendency to split up into a multitude of communities all jealously bent on preserving their citizenship and their political and legal prerogatives; on the other, the presence of numerous foreigners, both Greek and non-Greek, all engaged in cross-border trading. Conflict had to be overcome to make trading not only possible and efficient but also attractive. The commercial sector thus became the chief domain for various forms of public intervention. These took shape as early as the archaic period, and over the subsequent centuries they diversified greatly. Some measures targeted private individuals; others applied to particular products, above all grain. Their evolution led to overlaps and superpositions that make this whole matter particularly complex. Without entering into detailed descriptions, let us consider first the measures taken with a view to regulating commerce and protecting traders, then the agreements concluded between states, and last the purchases that cities effected directly.

Market Controls

The earliest supervisory and disciplinary measures were introduced as early as the archaic period, in the course of which trading centers, the *agorai* and *emporia,* were concretely set in place. (See above, pp. 129 and 135–36.) In the classical period those measures became definitively established and thereafter underwent only adaptations made necessary by the expansion (or reduction) of trade. As Aristotle remarked in his *Politics* (1321b4–18), among the most important magistracies (*archai*), essential for the good administration of any city, and in particular for discipline (*eutaxia*) and order (*kosmos*), were those concerning the agora (*peri tēn agoran*). The role of these magistrates was to oversee business obligations and relations (*symbolaia*) and maintain order (*eukosmia*). Other authors drew attention to the duty of these magistrates to remain vigilant where market transactions were concerned, to ensure that order reigned and that buyers and vendors all acted in good faith. According to Demosthenes (*Against Leptines* 19) and Hyperides (*Against Athenogenes* 14), fourth-century Athens had passed a law banning fraudulent practices (*apseudein*) in the agora.

Indeed, as numerous inscriptions from the classical period onward testify, every single city had at least one *agoranomos*. As his title indicates, he would be assigned to the agora, where, in the same way as other magistrates, he would remain in charge for one year (or in some cases for three or four months). Large cities would appoint several *agoranomoi,* and, as we shall see, Athens, because it was so huge, had to divide up their duties among a number of specialized posts. At another level, every *emporion* was subject to similar surveillance. *Epimelētai* responsible for the management of an *emporion* are known in a number of trading cities: these include Athens, Miletus, Rhodes and (after 166) Delos. Their tasks were to apply the laws, receive complaints and denunciations, intervene in a conciliatory capacity in altercations between vendors and purchasers, and, in all, to protect the interests of all. The official titles of these magistrates might vary from city to city (in Thasos, for example, the men who policed the port were known as *apologoi*), but cities of a modest size would simply assign tasks to their *agoranomoi,* who thus adjudicated both in the agoras and in the *emporia.* All these magistrates maintained regular contact with the tax farmers (known as *telōnai*), whose job it was to examine the statements made by merchants and the estimates of their wares (see above, p. 50) and who were also in a position to help the magistrates detect frauds. From the classical period onward, or possibly even earlier, all these controls had to be recorded in writing on a daily basis. Numerous sources attest the existence of a variety of documents from the fourth century B.C. onward. Some, such as the magistrates' registers, were public, while others, such as contracts, statements, inventories, and the shipping papers of traders and shipowners, were private.

No text is as explicit about market discipline as *The Athenian Constitution* (51) written by Aristotle or one of his followers. Its description is clearly of fourth-century Athens, but the synthesis is, mutatis mutandis, valid for all the Greek cities (Austin and Vidal-Naquet, no. 89):

> Also Market-controllers are elected by lot, five for Piraeus and five for the city (*asty*). To these the laws assign the superintendence of all merchandise, to prevent the sale of adulterated and spurious articles. Also, ten Controllers of Measures are appointed by lot, five for the city and five for Piraeus, who superintend all weights (*stathma*) and measures (*metra*), in order that sellers may use just ones (*dikaia*). Also there used to be ten Corn-Wardens elected by lot, five for Piraeus and five for the city, but now there are twenty for the city and fifteen for Piraeus. Their duties are first to see that unground corn (*sitos argos*) in the market is on sale at a fair (*dikaiōs*) price and next that millers sell barley-meal (*alphita*) at a price (*timai*) corresponding with that of barley (*krithai*) and baker-women loaves (*artoi*) at a price (*timai*) corresponding with that of wheat (*pyroi*) and weighing the amount (*stathmos*) fixed by the officials (*sitophylakes*)—for the law orders that these shall fix the weights. They elect by lot ten Port-Superintendents, whose duty is to superintend the harbour-markets and to compel the traders (*emporoi*) to bring to the city (*asty*) two-thirds of the sea-borne corn (*sitos*) that reaches the corn-market (*sitikon emporion*). (Translated by H. Rackham, The Loeb Classical Library, 1935)

Seen here is the Athenians' painstaking detail in legislation regarding grain (barley and wheat), the importation of which was vital. (See above, pp. 134–35.) Not only was there a special *sitikon emporion* in Piraeus, where all cargoes of *sitos* were unloaded and stored, but by law all imported grain had to be sold in Athens (and not transported further afield): two-thirds of it in the town of Athens, one-third in Piraeus itself, no doubt in proportion to their respective populations. The grain agoras also accommodated small-scale traders, *sitopōlai,* who specialized in cereal products and are mentioned in other texts. Finally, special magistrates, *sitophylakes* or "grain guardians" (ten of them in normal times but thirty-five in the years between 330 and 320, when there were grave shortages), were responsible for checking the correct prices of grain, barley flour, and loaves of wheaten bread and also the weight of the loaves, which they were empowered to fix. In accordance with a custom observed in the West for centuries, not only throughout antiquity but right down to the modern period, it was not the price of a loaf of bread that varied but its weight (in other words its size), which depended on the price of wheat. This *artos* was more rare and more expensive than barley flour or *maza,* and many people produced it in their own homes. (See above, pp. 95–96.) According to Lysias, (*Against the Grain Merchants* 5–6), the Athenian *sitophylakes* were also responsible for seeing that the *sitop⁻olai* did not purchase more than a stipulated quantity (50 *phormoi*), probably per day, when the grain arrived in the agora. This measure was designed to prevent hoarding and speculation.

All the other cities, albeit with more modest means and no doubt variable degrees of rigor, must have instituted similar controls over the quality, quantity, price, and weight of the products sold in their agoras. A number of sources mention a public building known as an *agoranomion,* which was where the *agoranomoi* worked. It was usually here that the city's official scales, weights, and measures would be kept, serving as standards for individual traders. The *agoranomoi* (or their equivalents) possessed the authority to intervene not only when complaints were lodged but also on their own initiative; and Aristotle alludes, somewhat vaguely, to their sanctioning powers (*Politics* 1322a13–15).

Texts from Athens and Miletus refer specifically to agora rules (*agoranomikoi nomoi*) and those governing *emporia* (*emporikoi nomoi*), but these must also have existed in other cities. Epigraphical texts carry traces of port regulations (Thasos) and of laws or other measures that fixed or modified the modalities of trade in certain commodities, such as wine and vinegar (Thasos), wool (Erythrae), and wood and charcoal (Delos). One particularly unusual text from Samos has survived. It dates from around 245/4 B.C. and introduces modifications to the regulations affecting four shops (*kapēleia*) installed within the precinct of the Sanctuary of Hera (*Heraion*), in particular the conditions of their leases, the restrictions imposed upon the tenants, and the provenance of their wares.

Price control was a matter that greatly exercised the Greeks, and it poses complex problems for a historian, problems that it is not possible to consider in detail in this short work. The text of *The Athenian Constitution* refers three times to the obligation to charge a fair price for unmilled grain, barley flour, and wheaten loaves of bread. But similar preoccupations must have arisen in connection with all kinds of products. Four inscriptions from the Hellenistic and Roman periods mention not only price controls but also the fixing of prices, in certain circumstances at least, in the context of local festivals in particular. Festivals drew exceptionally large crowds (see above, p. 130) that would set prices soaring. At some festivals, taxes were temporarily lifted. (See below, p. 155.) Three other inscriptions (from Delphi, Acraephia in Boeotia, and Athens) still preserve lists of prices (relating to fish and tripe). It seems that, by a vote in the assembly or even on the authority of the *agoranomoi,* cities had the power to cap prices, at least some of them, or even to fix maximum prices when circumstances demanded. So they clearly did not jib at authoritarian measures. Such texts are rare, however, and do not warrant any certain conclusions. In normal times, magistrates no doubt accepted the prices that the *emporoi* and *kapēloi* listed in their declarations. The prices would depend on the interplay of supply and demand and, in retail sales, could fluctuate as a result of bargaining. The text cited above indicates that the magistrates were in duty bound to repress abuses and ascertain that the margin of profit made by the retail vendors was a reasonable one (a detail that is confirmed by Lysias, *Against the Grain Merchants* 8). It thus seems that, in practice, the fixing of wholesale and retail prices depended primarily on negotiations between the merchants and the magistrates, and on the magistrates' power of persuasion.

That conclusion is confirmed, at least at the *emporion* level, by many inscriptions paying homage to the devotion of the *agoranomoi* or the generosity of *emporoi,* chiefly where grain was concerned, but sometimes regarding oil or other products, generally in periods of shortages and inflated prices. We find evidence of *agoranomoi,* other magistrates, or sometimes even the assembly itself exerting pressure on the *emporoi* to get them to sell at affordable prices—or even attempting to persuade the most altruistic (or the wealthiest) of them to sell their goods at a loss. Any price reductions obtained at higher levels would naturally be passed down to the retail level and would thereby affect competition. The ultimate aim or effect of such negotiations (although we possess no text to prove it) may have been to get the *emporoi* to agree to a single wholesale price for, for example, all grain of equal quality. So once again, it was a matter of negotiations and moral pressures rather than authoritarian measures.

This was the field of euergetism and benefactions, where an important role was played by the personal relations between influential citizens and wealthy *emporoi*. Generosity would peak when merchants agreed to deliver either their entire cargoes or part of them at no cost to the city. The foodstuffs would then become public property and could be resold at low prices or distributed free to all citizens (although not to other categories of inhabitants). In the Roman period this situation changed, and distributions of food would be made sometimes to the poorer strata of the population, sometimes, on the contrary, to privileged groups of *sitometroumenoi*. In both cases, it was the city, that is to say the assembly, that fixed the conditions, in particular the maximum quantity to be received by each individual or, if the goods were to be sold, the retail price. A similar situation obtained when the city itself bought provisions. (See below, pp. 166–69.)

Protectionist Measures

In his *Life of Solon* (24.1), Plutarch attributes various economic measures to the Athenian lawgiver, in particular a ban on the exportation of all products (*ginomena*) from Attica, with the exception of oil, on pain of public execration. This measure has been much discussed and has often been interpreted as an attempt to protect grain supplies. It may well have been just that, even at the beginning of the sixth century B.C., for Athens was already producing large quantities of oil and was soon to introduce strict measures concerning the importation of grain. As we have seen (p. 146), a law passed in the second half of the fourth century obliged *emporoi* to sell on the spot all cargoes of grain arriving in Piraeus. In the same period—between about 340 and 320, to be more precise—a number of orators' legal speeches referred to another law, the text of which is cited in Demosthenes' *Against Lacritus* 51 (Austin and Vidal-Naquet, no. 82). This law applied not to *xenoi* but to Athenians and metics and even individuals whose guardians (*kyrioi*) were Athenian or metics, for these could no doubt serve as intermediaries. The law is formulated negatively. It forbids the individuals to whom it is addressed to lend money for any ship not carrying to Athens grain or any other designated merchandise. (The sense of the last words is not clear.) In other words, the citizens of Athens were keen to steer most maritime loans (see above, p. 139) toward the maintenance of supplies of grain and other foodstuffs judged to be essential. However, it would be risky to read too much into this law, for it was passed in a period of shortages and uncertain provisioning.

We find other cities taking similar measures with a view to prohibiting the export of local grain in moments of need, for example in Thrace and the Hellespont, which was then (between 240 and 220) under Lagid control, and in the Achaean Confederation and Boeotia at the start of the second century. However, we do not know the duration of the public execration aimed by Teos in about 470 at, among others, those who impeded the importation of grain or tried to transfer imported grain elsewhere, either overland or by sea. The same applies to the law that Selymbria, a city on the Propontis, passed around 360 B.C. forbidding all exports of grain.

Grain was, without a doubt, a major preoccupation for the Greek cities. But we possess a curious law passed in Thasos, concerning not grain but wine. The text is not fully preserved, but, among diverse measures concerning the production and sale of the local wine, which enjoyed an excellent reputation in the Greek world (see above, p. 87), we read, "Let no Thasian ship import foreign wine between Athos and Pacheiē." The designated zone was vast, corresponding by and large to the whole Thracian Sea and containing a long coastal sector with a whole string of ports that Thasos was in a position to control. Clearly, the city wished to protect its own wine trade, but the wording of this law is surprising, since it applies exclusively to Thasian vessels (owned, no doubt, by Thasians) and we do not know whether there was any clause, now lost, applying to foreign ships. This piece of legislation probably dates from the 390s B.C., a time when Thasos had resumed control of the mainland zone (see above, p. 103), set up a new democracy, and undertaken far-reaching reforms in a number of different domains. So it was passed in a very particular context, possibly in response to transitory circumstances.

The Protection of Foreigners

At a very early date it became necessary to devise means to help and protect foreigners (*xenoi*), particularly those who moved from one city to another trading their wares. Throughout antiquity, links of hospitality (*xenia*) between families based in different cities and regions constituted networks, providing friendship and assistance. These facilitated trading, initially no doubt between high-ranking figures (see above, pp. 137–38), but eventually also between merchants of lower social standing. For example, Andocides (*On His Return* 11) tells of how the links his father had established with King Archelaus of Macedon in 411 procured him permission to fell as much wood as he wished in the royal forests and then take wooden oars to the Athenian fleet installed at Samos, selling them (to the city) at cost, that is to say at the price of their felling and transport. But a host might also lend money to a protégé, soften up his creditors, or deflect an attempt to seize his wares. Or he could be of assistance to a visiting merchant in the public domain if, for instance, some legal problem arose, for he could serve as the merchant's intermediary and guarantor. Such an intervention among the host's fellow citizens of course remained in the private domain, but it could nevertheless influence a political or legal decision. For centuries, links such as these continued to count for a great deal, but, as international relations and commerce developed, they turned out to be increasingly inadequate.

As early as the archaic period, a public institution known as *proxenia* extended *xenia* without replacing it. Any city could designate *proxenoi* among the citizens of other cities with which it was in contact. A *proxenos* became a kind of public host, responsible for welcoming and assisting any inhabitant of the city that had appointed him to his position. The *proxenos,* then, acted as an intermediary, protector, and patron to the foreigner. The official nature of his post conferred added authority upon his interventions among his fellow citizens, but he played no strictly juridical role. His responsibilities were heavy, but in exchange, over and above his title as a benefactor (*euergetēs*), a *proxenos* would always be granted a number of privileges. (Examples are provided in the next section of the present chapter.) Over the centuries, this institution developed considerably, chiefly due to the expansion of networks of contacts and trade from the Hellenistic period onward. Contrary to the claims of certain scholars, it was not gradually transformed into a purely honorific function. For as long as the institution lasted, the duties that accompanied *proxenia* continued to be very real.

A city could also offer asylum (*asylia*) to foreigners who visited it frequently. In the event of litigious proceedings within its territory, it would then protect them against any threat of seizure (*sylan*) of their goods. (See above, pp. 26–27.) Asylum, like *xenia,* was an ancient institution, often accompanied by the granting of security (*asphaleia*) for both the person and the possessions of the beneficiary, particularly in times of warfare. Many decrees from the fourth century onward spell out the details of the security offered: "security for himself and his goods, on both land and sea, in times of both war and peace"; or "the right to enter the port and leave it without fear of seizure (*asylei*) in times of peace and, outside truce periods (*aspondei*), in times of war." Clearly, such measures favored traders' freedom of movement.

As for altercations between citizens and foreigners that needed to be settled legally, as we shall see below (pp. 157–66), cities sometimes concluded bilateral agreements. But in the mid-fourth century B.C., the Athenians, on their own initiative, created a new institution for rapid settlement of legal disputes relating to the Piraeus *emporion.* A new procedure made it possible for any foreigner, whether domiciled in Athens (a metic) or not (a *xenos*), not only himself to bring a lawsuit known as a *dikē emporikē,* but furthermore to obtain justice within one month. In the domain of commerce, such speed was obviously intended to facilitate trade, but this decision may be partly explained by its context: there were more and more *xenoi* traders operating in Piraeus; and Athens had just lost the Social War, along with its empire. It is not known how long this institution lasted.

Personal Privileges

When citizens passed decrees granting personal privileges to individuals who had rendered them services, it was usually to thank and honor them. Such privileges included not only *proxenia,* the title of benefactor, and *asylia* (see above, previous section), but others too, such as citizenship (*politeia*), the right to own property (*enktèsis*), exemption from taxes (*ateleia*), assimilation into the citizens' own fiscal system (*isoteleia*), and so on. Such privileges came in diverse combinations, and varied according to the merits of the beneficiary. Some privileges brought political as well as economic advantages, but so long as beneficiaries did not make use of them, these remained purely honorific.

However, fiscal exemptions obviously affected trade. They might be either total or partial (that is to say applicable only to certain taxes, as would be spelled out), and, like *asylia,* they were of course applicable only within the limits of the city granting them. In some cases they were granted to specific groups, for instance colonists or military men who had come to settle on the city's territory, or to the members of a neighboring community that had been annexed (*sympoliteia*). In such cases they would often be partial and would usually be provisional, as they were designed primarily to facilitate the integration of newcomers. An economic motive appears more clearly in an *ateleia* decreed at the time of a festival. (See above, p. 148.) In these circumstances, the citizens hoped to attract as many people as possible by forgoing the benefit of taxes so as to offer affordable prices. Even if their primary aim (to insure the success of their festival) was of a political or religious order, this was a way of encouraging trade, thereby benefiting local merchants in particular. It may be that in such circumstances the *ateleia* customarily accompanied a capping of prices (see above, p. 148), but we possess no conclusive evidence on this matter. Most tax exemptions, however, were offered to individuals, many of whom were merchants who had themselves sometimes requested them. The advantages and facilities that they obtained encouraged them to return to the city as regularly as possible, bringing with them products the city needed. So this was a way for citizens to win the merchants' services.

In exceptional circumstances, entire cities might be granted *ateleia* by another state. For instance, after the 227 B.C. earthquake that destroyed part of the city of Rhodes, the tyrants Hiero and Gelo, along with King Seleucus III, offered *ateleia* to all Rhodian seamen (most of whom were traders) who would take their cargoes to Syracuse and to the Seleucid kingdom (Polybius, V.88.7 and 89.8). The tax exemption certainly included customs dues and port taxes, but this measure was probably no more than temporary. Another example is provided by Delos, which was declared to be *atelēs* in 166 B.C. (Polybius, XXX.31.10) and remained so to an unknown date, the privilege having been renewed in 58. This measure probably applied to the *emporion* and therefore to dues and taxes as in the case cited above, but in Delos it extended to all the merchants who went there. The tax-free status was conferred by a decision of the Roman Senate, for reasons as much political as economic, and it contributed greatly to the commercial rise of Delos. (See above, p. 133.)

There are other examples of the granting of collective privileges. But they resulted from negotiations and agreements concluded between particular states.

International Agreements

As we have seen (p. 35), Aristotle advised statesmen to keep an eye on exports (*exagōgē*) and imports (*eisagōgē*) and, in this connection, stressed the usefulness of treaties (*synthēkai*) and agreements (*symbolai*). So from the classical period onward at least, these preoccupations were familiar to the collective of citizens. There are many examples of agreements of this kind. The most ancient of them have left no traces, for they were probably concluded orally, before witnesses and with the swearing of reciprocal oaths. But texts engraved in stone appeared by the early classical period and became more frequent thereafter, above all in the Hellenistic period, together with literary evidence. Not all these agreements were recorded officially, but (to judge by the texts that have come down to us) when they were, it was either in juridical documents or in political treaties. Here are two examples of *ateleia* negotiated between cities and monarchical states.

In the early fourth century B.C., Athens established friendly relations with the princes who controlled the regions and cities of the Cimmerian Bosporus. The land there produced an abundance of grain, probably even the high-quality type of wheat that was suitable for making good bread (*artos*). Three speeches, strung out between around 400 and 325, the most explicit of which is Demosthenes' *Against Leptines* (31–33) (Austin and Vidal-Naquet, no. 81), allude to the privileges granted by the princes: the right to export (*exagōgē*) grain from the two *emporia* of Panticapaeum and Theodosia, loading priority for ships bound for Athens, and exemption from the one-thirtieth (3.33 percent) exit tax. In return, the princes were offered encomia, crowns, *ateleia,* and Athenian citizenship—all purely honorific benefits—and also the right to recruit oarsmen in Athens, at least from 347/6 onward, according to one honorific decree (Rhodes and Osborne, no. 64). No formal agreement appears to have been concluded: the princes simply offered the privileges (*dōreiai*), and the Athenians passed the decrees. It seems that this agreement had to be renewed whenever there was a change of ruler. The decree of 347/6 was certainly passed soon after the death of Leukon I.

The *ateleia* obtained by Miletus during the period 167–160 B.C. was even more remarkable. We know of it from a decree voted in honor of Eirenias, an eminent citizen whom the city had sent as an ambassador to the Seleucid court (Burnstein, no. 40). Over and above gifts of wheat, of wood for the construction of a gymnasium, and possibly of other forms of generosity now obliterated from the inscription, Eirenias obtained from the king *ateleia* for all products (*genēmata*) exported from the territory of Miletus (*ek tēs Milēsias*) to the kingdom, in other words exemption from the royal customs dues. It is clear that the exemption applied to products, not to merchants. The term *genēmata* in general designated produce from the land. In this case it was probably a matter of wine and oil, which Miletus produced in abundance, but wool and the famous products of its textile industry may also have been included. (See above, p. 99.) Now, at this date the city of Miletus was free and was the neighbor of the kingdom of Pergamum, which (ever since 188) had occupied most of western Asia Minor. In taking such an initiative, the city of Miletus was seeking facilities for maritime exports to a distant kingdom. We do not know what advantages the king derived from this arrangement, apart from the city's support and the honors the Milesians voted to bestow upon him, which in themselves were not negligible. But the citizens were at pains to stress the benefits that accrued to them, namely "an increase in the revenues (*prosodoi*) of the city and all its inhabitants." As in the preceding example, no formal agreement was drawn up.

After due negotiation and agreement, *asylia* could also be conferred upon an entire citizenry by people who practiced piracy, such as the Aetolians and the Cretans. (See above, p. 25.) This would guarantee reparation for illicit seizures. In the Hellenistic period, territorial *asylia* also developed. Cities and kings would sometimes recognize the *asylia* of a sanctuary or even an entire city together with its territory. Generally this answered to the city's desire to develop its festivals and local celebrations, as in the case of Magnesia-on-the-Maeander in 207/6 (Burnstein, no. 30 and 31), or to protect itself against piracy, as in the case of Teos a few years later (Burnstein, no. 33). Such *asylia* boosted the honor of a city and its local deity, and also resulted in attracting more merchants, pilgrims, and visitors in general. Finally, *asylia* could also be exchanged between two cities, with proper mutual juridical agreements; the two small cities of Oiantheia and Chaleion, in Locris, made such a concord in fifth century B.C., as did Miletus and Sardis in the second half of the fourth century. The latter arrangement is known to us from a Milesian decree where one clause runs, "Let access to Miletus be guaranteed to any Sardian who seeks it, without fear of seizure and even in periods when no truce exists, for those disembarking as well as those reembarking, for both individuals and for their goods that are being imported or exported; let access to Sardis and security be granted to any Milesian seeking this in similar conditions."

In the same way, juridical agreements gradually came to allow foreigners access to courts and set out the procedures to be followed. Through indirect allusions and fragments of inscriptions dating from the mid-fifth century to the mid-second B.C., we know of twenty or so agreements concluded between Athens and allied cities (as long as the Athenian empire lasted) and between Athens and more distant cities. These agreements were known at first as *symbolai,* then as *symbola.* A few examples of *symbola* are also known elsewhere; they date from around the same period (down to the early second century). Several were concluded between neighboring cities or ones with common borders, such as Miletus and Priene in Ionia, and Gortyn and Lato in Crete. The texts that have been preserved display perfect symmetry in the mutual definitions of rights and procedures. The institution was typically Greek in that it presupposed a homogeneous framework allowing each city to recognize the jurisdiction of the other. From the second century B.C. onward, it fell into disuse, for cities came to prefer to call in judges from foreign cities to resolve juridical differences.

Asylia agreements and *symbola,* concluded with a view to protecting the circulation of both individuals and goods, produced direct consequences for trade. It is remarkable that, apart from those agreements, we possess no examples of documents devoted exclusively to commercial relations. When such preoccupations do figure in formal agreements, it is always within the framework of treaties or political accords: the former, usually called *synthēkai*, created alliances (*symmachiai*) and proclaimed or renewed friendship (*philia*) between two contracting cities; the latter were conventions of *isopoliteia* by which two cities granted each other the right of potential citizenship; yet others combined both these two features. From the point of view of commercial relations, the most interesting documents are conventions of *isopoliteia*. Here, in chronological order, are a few examples of such agreements, selected from amongst the most explicit and significant of them.

Around 450, the two neighboring Cretan cities of Knossos and Tylissos concluded a treaty, probably putting an end to hostilities between the two. The text, which is not well preserved, is not easy to understand. Included among various clauses relating to cults, mutual assistance in times of warfare, sharing of booty, exchange of embassies, the location of frontiers, and the Tylissians' right to own real estate in Knossos, we find the following clause: "Let there be exports from Knossos to Tylissos and from Tylissos to Knossos; but if they are exported beyond Knossos, the same taxes as those of Knossians must be paid." The return of peace thus made it possible for trade between the two cities to resume (overland, given their proximity); and no doubt customs dues were reestablished. (The text does not allude to any taxes.) Each city retained the freedom to export to other places, but if the Tylissians did so through Knossos, they had to pay the same taxes as the Knossians (Austin and Vidal-Naquet, no. 8).

In 432 or 423/2 (the date is unclear), Athens concluded an alliance with Perdiccas, the king of Macedon. The text is very dilapidated, but it is possible to make out that Perdiccas granted the Athenians the sole right to export wood for oars. Wood, a strategic material, was offered to cities by various kings, particularly in the Hellenistic period. We know that in 411, under Perdiccas's successor, Andocides was able to fell all the wood he wished in the royal forests and to send wood to be made into oars for the Athenian fleet. (See above, pp. 152–53.) No doubt the treaty concluded twenty years earlier served as a background to this gift, and it was probably still valid in 407/6 when the Athenians voted a decree in honor of the king, offering him the titles of *proxenos* and *euergetēs* because he had given them wood and wood for oars, and (possibly) had authorized them to build triremes on the spot.

In 393/2, the *koinon* (confederation) of the cities of Chalcidice concluded a treaty in its turn with Amyntas III of Macedon; this lasted for fifty years. The confederation undertook not to conclude alliances with other cities in the region without the king's permission. In exchange, the king allowed the export, upon payment of the prescribed taxes, of pitch and wood for building of all categories, including shipbuilding—even pine wood, if the *koinon* needed it specifically and on condition that it gave the king advance warning. A further, more general clause gave the partners the right to trade between each other and also to sell elsewhere all other products, provided they paid the prescribed taxes (Rhodes and Osborne, no. 12). Clearly, what interested them above all were strategic materials.

At the beginning of the second century (in 185/4?), Miletus concluded an alliance combined with an *isopoliteia* with Heraclea-by Latmos, and then another (in 180) with Magnesia-on-the-Maeander (Burnstein, no. 37). Both these agreements ended a war, and both reflected Miletus's policy of expansion and extending its influence. They included clauses providing for *ateleia* for the circulation of material goods, slaves, and livestock that their owners might wish to evacuate in the event of warfare or danger and move to safety in the partner city. The first treaty also granted pasturing rights, untaxed, on the public land of Heraclea, to foreigners who owned land in the territory of Miletus, but it seems to have excluded specialized stock-raisers.

Similar clauses appear in several Cretan treaties, with the difference that the granting of pasturing rights was mutual. This group of texts comprises six alliance treaties and two *isopoliteia* conventions. The most ancient text goes back to the early third century. The rest fall into two groups, one from the late third century or early second, the other from between 111 and 109. The texts in the second group also created *isopoliteia* agreements. Ten different cities figure in these treaties, but Gortyn, Olous, Lato, and Hierapytna each appear more than once. The treaties reflect the well-known unrest in Crete, which abated at the end of the second century following the expansion of the larger cities at the expense of the weaker ones. Every one of these six treaties contained one remarkable clause, repeated almost word for word, which authorized trading in all products between the citizens of the two contracting cities, excluding the payment of taxes for overland trade but requiring payment of the port charges each city imposed on maritime trading. Three treaties, one from the first group, the others from the second, added one condition: both partners had to swear that the products purchased were destined for their own use (not for resale). Two of the agreements even state that citizens would have the right to sell to and buy from the partner citizens, to lend them money and borrow it from them, and to agree on any other transactions with them that conformed with the existing laws in both cities.

According to some scholars, these texts illustrate the desire of cities to stimulate trade. In truth, the alliances of Athens and of the Chalcidians with Macedon did have above all a strategic purpose. In all the other cases, it was a matter of restoring business relations following a conflict that had hindered or disrupted them and, in some, even of imposing quite strict limits upon those relations. In such contexts, commercial clauses clearly played no more than a secondary role. The primary objective of alliance treaties was certainly to establish or reestablish peace and to provide for mutual assistance in the event of conflicts with other states. Conventions of *isopoliteia* were to regulate the arrival and integration of new citizens, that is to say citizens from one partner city moving to the other, attracted either by more activity or by allures tendered out of concern to remedy the weakening of a civic body. Commercial clauses thus applied to citizens from the partner city as foreigners passing through, to whom they offered special advantages. This distinction has not always been understood. In any case, it is important to emphasize that most treaties and conventions contained no commercial arrangements at all.

However, many conventions of *isopoliteia* were concluded in a climate of peace. These therefore reflect the efforts cities were making to facilitate the circulation of individuals and goods more accurately than the alliance treaties do. Admittedly, some inscriptions are extremely laconic and refer to the granting of *ateleia,* for example, with but a single word, without giving any details. But others are more explicit. For example, in the first half of the fourth century (before 363/2), Histiaea in northern Euboea and the island of Ceos, whose cities then formed a single political unit (a *sympoliteia*), granted each other identical importation and exportation conditions, along with security for the traders involved. In the last third of the fourth century, the *isopoliteia* concluded between Miletus and Olbia, its colony on the Black Sea, allowed not only for recourse to the people's court (*dēmotikon dikastērion*) in the event of a business conflict (*symbolaion*), but also for tax exemption in both cities upon entering or leaving the port, except for citizens domiciled elsewhere than Miletus or Olbia (Rhodes and Osborne, no. 93). In both these cases, the partners were already on good terms and simply wished to increase their trade. Indeed, without special forms of protection (see above, pp. 152–56), trade was really possible only between friendly cities. But even when good relations were already well established, cities clearly preferred to include commercial clauses within wider agreements.

The existence of that practice, however, does not mean that all regional and long-distance trade had to be regulated by political or juridical agreements. On the contrary, in normal circumstances, that is to say in times of peace or in areas where peace reigned, private trading went ahead freely, needing no more than such measures as established frameworks, protection, and encouragement. (See above, p. 150–60.) Merchants were organized into associations and established relations with distant partners: in the Black Sea area, for instance. They would also choose their own particular regions and preferred trading networks (see above, p. 136) and thus became familiar with the needs of local markets. Freedom of the seas and of trade was a principle that clearly went without saying for the Greeks. This is proved by numerous texts, even if it was never proclaimed as a right. A law passed in Rhodes in the early Hellenistic period, when the city was at the peak of its power, is adduced in this connection. It is thought to have comprised a number of rules affecting maritime law, rules that Mediterranean seafarers tacitly accepted. In truth, all we have are late echoes of those rules. These appear first in Roman jurisprudence concerning the dumping overboard of merchandise in the event of danger, and later in medieval texts that introduced a number of new elements. It is impossible to form a clear idea of the scope of the Greeks' maritime rules or to reconstruct their content.

In general, private trade sufficed to meet current needs, at least in normal times. When it did not meet them adequately, cities would sometimes step in to supplement it, by making their own purchases.

Public Purchases

Cities and sanctuaries clearly made purchases and spent money to further their own projects. (See above, pp. 51–52 and 100.) Given the scarcity of gold, silver, copper, and tin mines in the Mediterranean region, in order to mint coins, most cities had to buy metal from outside (or reuse foreign coins, melting them down or overstamping them). Even in the most famous cases, Athens and Thasos, we do not know in what conditions or at what price cities procured the silver and gold produced by private entrepreneurs from their own mines. The construction and upkeep of warships and the building and restoration of public edifices and sacred monuments required stone, marble, wood, iron, lead, pitch, various dyes such as red ochre, and such other materials as hemp and linen—materials that cities could not always find to hand or in domains that they controlled. All cities regularly sold locally goods confiscated from individuals, and sometimes even public property such as land that they wished to offload. These sales were organized by vendors (*pōlētai*), magistrates appointed for one year and made responsible for renting out public and sacred land and buildings, and also for farming out taxes and other similar operations, all of which the Greeks regarded as sales (Aristotle, *The Athenian Constitution* 47.2–5).

All the above transactions were limited to well-defined sectors, and public purchases were arranged by private commercial intermediaries. But where certain other products were imported by the cities themselves, at their own expense, it was quite a different matter. From the fourth century B.C. onward, increasingly numerous inscriptions refer to public purchases of grain and, sometimes, oil. Such purchases took place chiefly in times of shortages, when provisioning was difficult and prices were inflated (all interconnected problems), but no doubt they also occurred in normal times, when privately arranged imports proved insufficient. Some cities would designate a buyer of grain (*sitōnēs*) or of oil (*elaiōnēs*) or possibly several at once, depending on the circumstances. They would entrust a sum taken from the public funds to these officials and commission them to seek out oil or grain from abroad and import it at the lowest possible price. The task of these men was completed when they returned and the cargo, which was public property (several texts refer specifically to *sitos dēmosios*), was either sold on to retailers or distributed freely, in accordance with conditions laid down by the assembly in the same way as conditions applying to gifts from *euergetai*. (See above, p. 150.) It is not hard to imagine (although we do not know for certain) how the *sitōnai* and the *elaiōnai* would set about their task. Even if they themselves did not operate as traders or shipowners, they would probably know of wholesalers with whom they could do business, which would no doubt involve a maritime loan. (See above, p. 139.) In all likelihood, they would not themselves go on the voyage, but they may sometimes have done so, the better to protect the interests of the city.

If they found *emporoi* willing to lower their prices, they may even have managed to buy the goods on the spot. Purchases like these were certainly more frequent than is indicated by our sources. We may assume, for example, that the city of Athens itself would sometimes buy grain from the princes of the Cimmerian Bosporus, through the links it had fostered with them. Sometimes when a situation became intolerable, devoted *agora-nomoi* or other magistrates would themselves take the initiative to buy grain or oil at their own expense and offer the goods to the city, which would then proceed in the usual fashion. Such gestures of largesse became increasingly numerous from the Hellenistic period onward, as euergetism became more common.

As early as the fourth century, some cities took steps to make it permanently possible to buy grain at their own expense by creating a regular deposit of funds (*sitōnikon*) and each year appointing a *sitōnes* or several *sitōnai,* who thus filled public posts just as magistrates did. This institution progressively spread, and by the first century A.D. it seems to have been a regular feature of the Asia Minor cities. The initial deposit of funds might come from a *euergetēs* or be amassed by a general appeal for contributions, for example. If the grain was then resold, the fund would regularly renew itself. If the money was invested in the form of loans offered to private individuals, the interest obtained would regularly be used for buying grain. No institution of this kind is known for oil.

As for the metals for minting coins and the products necessary for public enterprises, cities were certainly concerned that these should be available. But to judge from the documents that have come down to us, these items were always imported by private individuals, except in one case: possibly in the wake of the frictions of 362 B.C. and Ceos's renewed membership in the

Second Athenian Alliance, the island's cities agreed to renew Athens' monopoly on the purchase of red ochre (Austin and Vidal-Naquet, no. 86; Rhodes and Osborne, no. 40). So even if the ochre from Ceos was shipped privately to Athens, it never came onto the market but instead immediately became Athenian property. It seems reasonable to suppose that other cities may occasionally have imported such strategic products as wood in a similar way, making the most of their relations with the kings of Macedon.

Such direct purchases are interesting in a number of respects. In the first place, they involved either goods for private consumption, such as vital grain or oil, or a strategic product for public use, such as the ochre from Ceos. Second, except in that last case, the purpose of the purchase was never to monopolize the product. The quantities of grain involved were relatively modest and were clearly considered no more than stopgaps. In a number of cases, they were sold or distributed on the occasion of some festival. In other cases, they were not used until the end of winter, when they helped citizens to keep going until the new crops were harvested. We even find that in Delos, at the beginning of the second century, and in Tauromenium from 110 to 90 and 81 to 61, the (large) funds reserved for purchasing grain were left unused in the public coffers for quite long periods. All the same, such purchases did have an indirect impact, for they created competition, whose result was to reduce the prices charged in private commerce. Sometimes grain was being sold at two different prices, that of the free market and that paid by the cities, which may be described as the official price. But sales and public distributions of this grain customarily took place in specifically designated places, in accordance with particular procedures, and under the direction of presiding magistrates.

The world of commerce was a complex one, in which activities taking place at different levels continued to operate alongside one another for centuries. The cities adopted a diversity of methods to supervise, protect, and encourage trade, or even, if necessary, to supplement it. In this domain, the Greeks clearly lacked neither interest nor imagination. Nevertheless, even if they did consider the well-being of all, as the Milesians declared he had when they honored Eirenias, it would be anachronistic to credit them with a policy for commercial development or even a veritable policy on imports. Such policies would have required more complete and coherent measures, in particular a more flexible taxation system. (See above, p. 54.) Even more clearly than in the production sector, we can see that the most constant preoccupation of Greek citizens was to safeguard their own supplies. (See above, pp. 63–65.)

PRIMARY TEXTS
Trade as Seen by a Philosopher

When currency had been now invented as an outcome of the necessary exchange of goods, there came into existence the other form of wealth-getting, trade (*kapēlikon*), which at first no doubt went on in a simple form, but later became more highly organized (*technikōteron*) as experience discovered the sources and methods of exchange that would cause most profit. Hence arises the idea that the art of wealth-getting deals specially with money, and that its function is to be able to discern from what source a large supply can be procured. [. . .] Hence people seek for a different definition of riches and the art of getting wealth, and rightly, for natural wealth-getting and natural riches are different: natural wealth-getting belongs to household management (*oikonomikē*), whereas the other kind belongs to trade (*kapēlikē*), producing wealth not indiscriminately but by the method of exchanging goods. It is this art of wealth-getting that is thought to be concerned with money, for money is the first element and limit of commerce. And these riches, that are derived from this art of wealth-getting, are truly unlimited. [. . .] But the household branch of wealth-getting has a limit, inasmuch as the acquisition of money is not the function of household management. Hence from this point of view it appears necessary that there should be a limit to all riches, yet in actual fact we observe that the opposite takes place; for all men engaged in wealth-getting try to increase their money to an unlimited amount.

> Aristotle, *Politics* 1257b1–34 (*passim*), translated by
> H. Rackham, The Loeb Classical Library, 1959

The Law (or Ruling) from Kyparissia, in Messenia, on Customs Dues (Fourth or Third Century B.C.)

God. Whoever imports items of merchandise into the territory of Kyparissia must, after landing them, declare them in writing to the receivers of the fiftieth and pay the fiftieth before taking anything away or selling it; if not, let him pay ten times [the tax]. Whatever is to be exported by sea, let it be loaded on board after presentation of a written declaration to the receivers of the fiftieth and payment of the fiftieth, after having called in the receiver before embarking; if not, let [the merchant] pay ten times the fiftieth, as is laid down by the rule. If anyone undervalues his merchandise, let the receiver confiscate it for the claimed sum, in conformity with the law.

> H. W. Pleket, *Epigraphica I: Texts on the Economic
> History of the Greek World,* no. 8 (Leiden, 1964)

*Extract (Lines 99–103) from the Regulations of the Mysteries
of Andania (Messene) (92 B.C.)*

Agora. Let the *hieroi* designate the place for all sales; let the agoranomos of the city make sure that the salesmen sell products that
are not adulterated or doctored and use weights and measures
that conform to the public weights and measures; let him fix neither the price nor the time of the sales and let no-one insist on
any dues from the salesmen for their pitch; if people do not abide
by these sales rules, let him whip the slaves and charge the free
men a fine of twenty drachmas, and let this judgement be made
by the *hieroi*.

N. Deshours, *Les Mystères d'Andania: Etude d'épigraphie et
d'histoire religieuse,* pp. 38–39 (Paris and Bordeaux, 2006)

Treaty Between the Aetolian Koinon *and the City of Trikka
in Thessaly (Late Third Century B.C.?)*

With good fortune. The *koinon* of the Aetolians has granted to
the city of Trikka citizenship, exemption from taxes, *asylia,* and
security for them and their goods on both land and sea, in both
times of war and times of peace. The Trikkaians have granted the
same privileges to the Aetolians. Phrikos, Menoitas, Dorkinas,
Skorpion, Koiseas, and Archidamos were members of the council. Pausias was the secretary.

H. Bengtson, *Die Staatsverträge des Altertums,* III,
no. 542 (Munich, 1969)

Conclusion

This book has attempted to show, within a few pages, how the ancient Greeks conceived of their economic activities and organized them within the framework of their cities. Describing characteristic features, sector by sector, it has endeavored, where possible, to sketch the evolution of production and trading, which seems to have been closely linked with the political changes and upheavals of the ancient world. A number of conclusions may be drawn from this rapid overview of the scene.

The first conclusion is really a general impression that emerges from a long-term view: over the centuries, production and trade certainly seem to have increased in the world of the cities. To be sure, progress was slow and irregular, passing through both highs and lows, and it always varied from one region to another and one social level to another, so it is not possible to quantify it. Nevertheless, that progress is detectable in a wide range of factors: demographic growth; the diffusion of minted money; the diversification of trades; the progress of urbanization, means of transport, and security, and also of reading, writing, and scientific knowledge; and the ancient world's progressive opening up to large political systems, culminating in the advent of a kind of golden age, thanks to the *pax Romana*. That is why certain scholars have tried to apply at least some modern criteria to the economic growth of the early Roman Empire in particular. Others, on the contrary, have strongly emphasized the limits of that growth, and several have even concluded that the economic development of the ancient world was a failure, above all because the cities, as public bodies, along with the Hellenistic kings and the Roman emperors, all remained indifferent to the material possibilities of their world and failed in the task of exploiting them for the greater good of all.

Certainly neither of those schools of thought have been short of arguments. But the very concept of growth is problematic. It cannot, in all seriousness, be applied to the ancient economy, even within the limits of one particular place or one particular period. In the first place, even the most elementary information is almost totally lacking. How and within what framework, for example, can we evaluate notions such as the gross domestic product or the standard of living of individuals? Furthermore, and above all, recourse to such recent concepts is manifestly anachronistic, for, consciously or not, it is basically inspired by the Formalist school of thought. We know full well that, even if the Greeks, both individually and collectively, could demonstrate know-how and inventiveness in meeting the needs of themselves and those around them, and in improving their tools and endeavoring to become richer, neither their philosophers nor the citizens, who were responsible for collective decisions, ever conceived of economic activities as a whole, with a view to promoting growth and general well-being.

A second, far more obvious conclusion is that the economy of ancient Greece was marked by great diversity and even by contradictory features, not only from one region or city to another, but in its very structures. On the one hand, it is clear that there were long periods when nothing much changed, which must, without passing any value judgments, be described as archaic or primitive. These were periods when agriculture predominated and the constraints of the natural environment were considerable, as were those of technology, of warfare and violence, and of the slow pace of movement and transport from one place to another. By reason of their fragility in the face of unexpected and imponderable events, production and trade would frequently falter. These periods were marked by a number of common characteristics: the conservatism of both mind-sets and institutions, in particular in the thinking of philosophers and the attitudes of citizens in their collective decisions; unequal rights and social conditions between citizens and foreigners, men and women, the free and the nonfree; and the exploitation of a servile and dependent workforce. For centuries, many cities remained small peasant country towns, more or less inward-looking and faithful above all to traditional life. Although these are the ones that we know least about, they probably represented the great majority of Greek cities. On the other hand, in other cities—the classic examples are Athens and Rhodes—where interactions between private initiative and public interventions produced a dynamic effect, a number of sectors of the economy became increasingly open to trade; and upstream this stimulated the production of both agriculture and the craft industries.

From the second half of the fifth century B.C. onward, a new spirit emerged in certain circles, one more attuned to efficient management methods, a quest for profits and productivity, and, eventually, a veritable grasp of big business, which spread progressively within the more affluent social strata.

Should we come, then, as some do, to a third conclusion: that, in the fourth century B.C. or even the second half of the fifth, a market economy appeared, at least in an embryonic state, and thereafter spread in cities such as Athens? To do so would be yet again to apply to the ancient economy a modern concept that cannot be taken for granted, and one often used in an equivocal way to boot. At an elementary level, it is clear that the Greek world was familiar with the idea of a market, not just in the material form of the agora and the *emporion,* but also in an abstract sense. Not only did several sectors of agriculture and the craft industries gear their production to market sales, but the law of supply and demand influenced the way prices developed. It is also true that economic development was linked with urban expansion, the diffusion of minted money, and the impact of credit. So the Greek cities did, for the first time in Western history, create a vast economic entity that was relatively homogeneous and was marked by free production and trading. But in the modern sense, that is to say in the language of economists, a market economy is a system in which the market is the mechanism that fuels and autoregulates the entire economy, even if certain marginal sectors elude it. Now, in the ancient world, much of production, indeed, probably most of it, always aimed for self-sufficiency at the level of the cities, and therefore at the level of the local markets. It was always dependent upon demand and never encountered any real competition.

Despite the diffusion of minted money, private and public hoarding was always rife. There never did exist a great market serving the entire ancient world or even the whole Mediterranean region, in which prices for the same products would be more or less the same everywhere and would all fluctuate together. Instead, there was a multitude of regional markets, all with their own networks and their own prices. Even the spirit of enterprise manifested by the wealthy and by some prominent citizens cannot strictly be qualified as capitalism *avant la lettre,* for conditions varied, and these men continued to think for the most part as landowners; specifically, they remained faithful to the values of real-estate ownership, leisure (*scholē*), and politics. And even though a labor market was created from time to time, chiefly by public enterprises, the Greek world as a whole never did know of such a thing.

To sum up the ancient economy in a single word, the term precapitalist or preindustrial is often used. It is quite true that the ancient economy does share features in common with the traditional economies of the West before the modern period and the industrial revolution. But that formula, established as a comparison and a negative one, does not get us very far. Not only does it confuse the whole of antiquity and the Middle Ages in a single entity, but it is also ambiguous: it may, on the one hand, define an economy that is different from our own, which is true enough, but on the other hand it can be applied to an early stage of capitalism and the industrial era, which in this case is false. In truth, it is pointless to try to reduce the economy of the Greek cities to a single formula or model, not only because it was marked by great diversity and contradictory features, but also because it evolved slowly in the course of a thousand years of history.

The situation was thus a complex one, as this book has tried to show. By and large, the Greek world experienced a mixed economy, that is to say one that operated simultaneously on two of the three levels that F. Braudel has recognized still to exist in the modern world: one at ground level, the elementary, traditional, partially self-sufficient production of rural agriculture and craftsmens' workshops, in short a subsistence economy; and a second at a higher level, with activities oriented rather toward trade, which, if one insists on formulated labels, might be described as a multimarket economy.

BIBLIOGRAPHY

ANCIENT TEXTS IN TRANSLATION

Austin, M.M., and P. Vidal-Naquet. Part 2 in *Economic and Social History of Ancient Greece: An Introduction.* Translated from the French by M.M. Austin. London, 1977.

Burstein, S.M. *The Hellenistic Age from the Battle of Ipsos to the Death of Kleopatra VII.* Cambridge, 1985.

Migeotte, L. *L'emprunt public dans les cités grecques.* Québec and Paris, 1984.

Pleket, H.W. *Epigraphica.* Vol. 1. *Texts on the Economic History of the Greek World.* Leiden, 1964.

Rhodes, P.J., and R. Osborne. *Greek Historical Inscriptions 404–323 B.C.* Oxford, 2003.

SECONDARY SOURCES

Alcock, S.E. *Graecia Capta: The Landscapes of Roman Greece.* Cambridge, 1993.

Amouretti, M.-C. "L'agriculture de la Grèce antique: Bilan des recherches de la dernière décennie." *Topoi Orient-Occident* 4 (1994): 69–94.

————, and G. Comet. *Hommes et techniques de l'Antiquité à la Renaissance*. Paris, 1993.

Aperghis, G. G. "A Reassessment of the Laurion Mines Lease Records." *Bulletin of the Institute of Classical Studies* 42 (1997–98): 1–20.

Archibald, Z. H., J. K. Davies, V. Gabrielsen, and G. J. Oliver, eds. *Hellenistic Economies*. London and New York, 2001.

————. *Making, Moving and Managing: The New World of Ancient Economies, 323–31 B.C.* Oxford, 2005.

Austin, M. M. "Society and Economy." In *The Cambridge Ancient History*, vol. VI, *The Fourth Century B.C.*, 2nd ed., edited by D. M. Lewis, J. Boardman, S. Hornblower, and M. Ostwald, 527–64. Cambridge, 1994.

————, and P. Vidal-Naquet. Part 1 in *Economic and Social History of Ancient Greece: An Introduction*. Translated from the French by M. M. Austin. London, 1977.

Balansard, A., ed. *Le travail et la pensée technique dans l'Antiquité classique: Lecture et relecture d'une analyse de psychologie historique de Jean-Pierre Vernant*. Ramonville and Saint-Agne, 2003.

Blondé, F., and A. Muller. "L'artisanat en Grèce ancienne: Les artisans, les ateliers." *Topoi Orient-Occident* (1998): 541–845.

Bogaert, B. *Banques et banquiers dans les cités grecques*. Leiden, 1968.

Braudel, F. *The Mediterranean and the Mediterranean World in the Age of Philip II*. Vol. 2. Translated by S. Reynolds. Berkeley and Los Angeles, 1995.

Bresson, A. *La cité marchande*. Bordeaux and Paris, 2000.

————. "Merchants and Politics in Ancient Greece: Social and Economic Aspects." In *Mercanti e politica nel mondo antico*, edited by C. Zaccagnini, 139–63. Rome, 2003.

————. "Ecology and Beyond: The Mediterranean Paradigm." In *Rethinking the Mediterranean*, edited by W. V. Harris, 94–114. Oxford, 2005.

————. "Coinage and Money Supply in the Hellenistic Age." In *Making, Moving and Managing: The New World of Ancient Economies, 323–31 B.C.*, edited by Z. H. Archibald, J. K. Davies, V. Gabrielsen, and G. J. Oliver, 44–72. Oxford, 2005.

————, and P. Rouillard, eds. *L'emporion.* Bordeaux and Paris, 1993.

Broughton, T. R. S. "Roman Asia Minor." In *An Economic Survey of Ancient Rome,* vol. IV, edited by T. Frank, 499–918. Baltimore, 1938.

Bruhns, H. "La cité antique de Max Weber." *Opus* 6–8 (1987–89): 29–42.

————, and J. Andreau, eds. *Sociologie économique et économie de l'Antiquité: À propos de Max Weber.* Cahiers du Centre de Recherches Historiques 34 (October 2004).

Brunet, M., ed. *Territoires des cités grecques: Actes de la table ronde internationale organisée par l'Ecole Française d'Athènes, 31 sept.–3 nov., 1991.* Athens and Paris, 1999.

Burford, A. *The Greek Temple Builders at Epidauros.* Liverpool, 1969.

————. *Craftsmen in Greek and Roman Society.* London, 1972.

————. *Land and Labour in the Greek World.* Baltimore and London, 1993.

Casson, L. *Ancient Trade and Society.* Detroit, 1984.

Chapman, A. "Karl Polanyi (1886–1964) for the Student." In *Autour de Polanyi: Vocabulaires, théories et modalités des échanges (Nanterre, 12–14 juin 2004),* edited by P. Clancier, F. Joannès, P. Rouillard, and A. Tenu, 17–32. Paris, 2005.

Christesen, P. "Economic Rationalism in Fourth-Century B.C.E. Athens." *Greece and Rome* 50 (2003): 31–56.

Cohen, E. E. *Athenian Economy and Society: A Banking Perspective.* Princeton, 1992.

Corbier, M. "City, Territory and Taxation." In *City and Country in the Ancient World,* edited by J. Rich and A. Wallace-Hadrill, 211–39. London and New York, 1991.

Crawford, M., ed. *Sources for Ancient History.* Cambridge, 1983.

Dalton, G., ed. *Primitive, Archaic and Modern Economies: Essays of K. Polanyi.* New York, 1968.

Davies, J. K. "Cultural, Social and Economic Features of the Hellenistic World." In *The Cambridge Ancient History,* vol. VII.1, *The Hellenistic World,* 2nd ed., edited by F. W. Walbank, A. E. Astin, M. W. Frederiksen, and R. M. Ogilvie, 257–320. Cambridge, 1984.

————. "Society and Economy." In *The Cambridge Ancient History,* vol. V, *The Fifth Century B.C.,* edited by D.M. Lewis, J. Boardman, J.K. Davies, and M. Ostwald, 287–305. Cambridge, 1992.

————. "Ancient Economies: Models and Muddles." In *Trade, Traders and the Ancient City,* edited by H. Parkins and C. Smith, 225–56. London and New York, 1998.

————. "Hellenistic Economies." In *The Cambridge Companion to the Hellenistic World,* edited by G.R. Bugh, 73–92. Cambridge, 2006.

de Callataÿ, F. "A Quantitative Survey of Hellenistic Coinages: Recent Achievements." In *Making, Moving and Managing: The New World of Ancient Economies, 323–31 B.C.,* edited by Z.H. Archibald, J.K. Davies, and V. Gabrielsen, 73–91. Oxford, 2005.

Etienne, R., C. Müller, and F. Prost. *Archéologie historique de la Grèce antique.* Paris, 2000.

Finley, M.I., ed. *Problèmes de la terre en Grèce ancienne.* Paris and The Hague, 1973.

————. *Economy and Society in Ancient Greece.* London, 1981.

————. *Ancient History: Evidence and Models.* London, 1985.

————. *The Ancient Economy.* Berkeley and Los Angeles, 1973. (New ed. 1999, with a foreword by I. Morris and the *Further Thoughts* of M.I. Finley.)

Foxhall, L. *Olive Cultivation in Ancient Greece: Seeking the Ancient Economy.* Oxford, 2007.

Fuks, A. *Social Conflict in Ancient Greece.* Jerusalem and Leiden, 1984.

Gabrielsen, V. *Financing the Athenian Fleet: Public Taxation and Social Relations.* Baltimore and London, 1994.

————. "Economic Activity, Maritime Trade and Piracy in the Hellenistic Aegean." *Revue des Etudes Anciennes* 103 (2001): 219–40.

————. "Banking and Credit Operations in Hellenistic Times." In *Making, Moving and Managing: The New World of Ancient Economies, 323–31 B.C.,* edited by Z.H. Archibald, J.K. Davies, V. Gabrielsen, and G.J. Oliver, 136–64. Oxford, 2005.

Gallant, T.W. *Risk and Survival in Ancient Greece: Reconstructing the Rural Domestic Economy.* Cambridge, 1991.

Garlan, Y. *War in the Ancient World: A Social History.* Translated by J. Lloyd. New York, 1975.

———. *Slavery in Ancient Greece.* Translated by J. Lloyd. Ithaca, 1988.

Garnsey, P., ed. *Non-Slave Labour in the Greco-Roman World.* Cambridge, 1980.

———. *Famine and Food Supply: Responses to Risk and Crisis.* Cambridge, 1988.

———. *Food and Society in Classical Antiquity.* Cambridge, 1988.

———, K. Hopkins, and C.R. Whittaker, eds. *Trade in the Ancient Economy.* London, 1983.

———, and C.R. Whittaker, eds. *Trade and Famine in Classical Antiquity.* Cambridge, 1983.

Gauthier, P. "De Lysias à Aristote (Ath. pol., 51, 4): Le commerce du grain à Athènes et les fonctions des sitophylaques." *Revue Historique de Droit Français et Etranger* 59 (1981): 5–28.

———. "Les saisies licites aux dépens des étrangers dans les cités grecques." *Revue Historique de Droit Français et Etranger* 60 (1982): 553–76.

———. "Grandes et petites cités: Hégémonie et autarcie." *Opus* 6–8 (1987–89): 187–97.

Greene, K. "Technological Innovation and Economic Progress in the Ancient World: M.I. Finley Reconsidered." *Economic History Review* 53 (2000): 29–59.

Hansen, M.-H. "The Hellenic Polis." In *A Comparative Study of Thirty City-State Cultures: An Investigation Conducted by the Copenhagen Polis Centre,* edited by M.-H. Hansen, 141–87. Copenhagen, 2000.

———. *Polis: An Introduction to the Ancient Greek City-State.* Oxford, 2006.

———. *The Shotgun Method: The Demography of the Ancient Greek City-State Culture.* Columbia, Missouri, and London, 2006.

Hanson, V.D. *The Other Greeks: The Family Farm and the Agrarian Roots of Western Civilization.* New York, 1995.

———. *Warfare and Agriculture in Classical Greece.* 2nd ed. Berkeley and Los Angeles, 1998.

Harris, E.M. "Workshop, Marketplace and Household: The Nature of Technical Specialization in Classical Athens and Its Influence on

Economy and Society." In *Money, Labour and Land: Approaches to the Economies of Ancient Greece,* edited by P. Cartledge, E. E. Cohen, and L. Foxhall, 67–99. London and New York, 2002.

Hodkinson, S. "Animal Husbandry in the Greek Polis." In *Pastoral Economies in Classical Antiquity,* edited by C. R. Whittaker, 35–74. Cambridge, 1988.

Hopkins, K. "Economic Growth and Towns in Classical Antiquity." In *Towns in Societies: Essays in Economic History and Historical Sociology,* edited by P. Abrams and E. A. Wrigley, 35–77. Cambridge, 1978.

———. "Introduction." In *Trade in the Ancient Economy,* edited by P. Garnsey, K. Hopkins, and C. R. Whittaker, ix–xxxv. London, 1983.

Hopper, R. J. *Trade and Industry in Classical Greece.* London, 1976.

Horden, P., and N. Purcell. *The Corrupting Sea: A Study of Mediterranean History.* Oxford, 2000.

Howgego, C. "Why Did Ancient States Strike Coins?" *Numismatic Chronicle* 1990: 1–25.

———. *Ancient History from Coins.* London and New York, 1995.

Howe, T. *Pastoral Politics: Animals, Agriculture and Society in Ancient Greece.* Claremont, 2008.

Humphreys, S. C. "History, Economics and Anthropology: The Work of Karl Polanyi." *History and Theory* 8 (1969): 165–212. (Reprint with Additional Note in *Anthropology and the Greeks,* 31–75. London, 1978.)

Isager, S., and J. E. Skydsgaard. *Ancient Greek Agriculture: An Introduction.* London and New York, 1992.

Kim, H. S. "Small Change and the Moneyed Economy." In *Money, Labor and Land: Approaches to the Economies of Ancient Greece,* edited by P. Cartledge, E. E. Cohen, and L. Foxhall, 44–51. London and New York, 2002.

Labarre, G., and M.-T. Le Dinahet. "Les métiers du textile en Asie Mineure de l'époque hellénistique à l'époque impériale." *Aspects de l'artisanat du textile dans le monde méditerranéen (Egypte, Grèce, monde romain),* 49–118. Lyon and Paris, 1996.

Larsen, J. A. O. "Roman Greece." In *An Economic Survey of Ancient Rome,* vol. 4, edited by T. Frank, 259–498. Baltimore, 1938.

Lawall, M.L. "Amphoras and Hellenistic Economies: Addressing the (Over)emphasis on Stamped Amphora Handles." In *Making, Moving and Managing: The New World of Ancient Economies, 323–31 B.C.,* edited by Z.H. Archibald, J.K. Davies, V. Gabrielsen, and G.J. Oliver, 188–232. Oxford, 2005.

Le Rider, G. *La naissance de la monnaie: Pratiques monétaires de l'Orient ancien.* Paris, 2001.

Leveau, P. "La ville antique, 'ville de consommation'?" *Etudes Rurales* Jan.–Sept. 1983, 275–89.

Lowry, S. Todd. *The Archeology of Economic Ideas: The Classical Greek Tradition.* Durham, 1987.

Manning, J.G., and I. Morris, eds. *The Ancient Economy: Evidence and Models.* Stanford, 2005.

Meadows, A., and K. Shipton. *Money and Its Uses in the Ancient Greek World.* Oxford, 2001.

Meiggs, R. *Trees and Timber in the Ancient Mediterranean World.* Oxford, 1982.

Meikle, S. *Aristotle's Economic Thought.* Oxford, 1995.

Migeotte, L. "Démocratie et entretien du peuple à Rhodes d'après Strabon (XIV, 2, 5)." *Revue des Etudes Grecques* 102 (1989): 515–28.

———. "Le pain quotidien dans les cités hellénistiques: À propos des fonds permanents pour l'approvisionnement en grain." *Cahiers du Centre G. Glotz* 2 (1991): 19–41.

———. "Les finances publiques des cités grecques: Bilan et perspectives de recherche." *Topoi Orient-Occident* 5 (1995): 7–32.

———. "Finances et constructions publiques." In *Stadtbild und Bürgerbild im Hellenismus,* edited by M. Wörrle and P. Zanker, 79–86. Munich, 1995.

———. "Les finances des cités grecques au-delà du primitivisme et du modernisme." In *ENERGEIA: Studies on Ancient History and Epigraphy Presented to H.W. Pleket,* edited by J.H.M. Strubbe, R.A. Tybout, and H.S. Versnel, 79–96. Amsterdam, 1996.

———. "Le contrôle des prix dans les cités grecques." In *Entretiens d'archéologie et d'histoire, 3: Prix et formation des prix dans les économies antiques,* edited by J. Andreau, P. Briant, and R. Descat, 33–52. St.-Bertrand-de-Comminges, 1997.

———. "La mobilité des étrangers en temps de paix en Grèce ancienne." In *La mobilité des personnes en Méditerranée de l'Antiquité à l'époque moderne: Procédures de contrôle et documents d'identification—La mobilité négociée,* edited by C. Moatti, 615–48. Rome, 2004.

———. "La gestion des biens sacrés dans les cités grecques." In *Symposion 2003: Vorträge zur griechischen und hellenistichen Rechtsgeschichte (Marburg, 30 September–4 Oktober 2003),* edited by G. Thür and H. A. Rupprecht, 235–48. Vienna, 2006.

———. "Les cités grecques: Une économie à plusieurs niveaux." In *L'économie antique, une économie de marché? Actes des deux tables rondes tenues à Lyon les 4 février et 30 novembre 2004,* edited by Y. Roman and J. Dalaison, 69–86. Paris, 2008.

Millett, P. *Lending and Borrowing in Ancient Athens.* Cambridge, 1991.

———. "Productive to Some Purpose? The Problem of Ancient Economic Growth." In *Economies Beyond Agriculture in the Classical World,* edited by D. J. Mattingly and J. Salmon, 17–48. London and New York, 2001.

Mitchell, S., and C. Katsari, eds. *Patterns in the Economy of Roman Asia Minor.* Swansea, 2005.

Moreno, A. *Feeding the Democracy: The Athenian Chain Supply in the Fifth and Fourth Centuries B.C.* Oxford, 2007.

Moreno, N. *Trade in Classical Antiquity.* Cambridge, 2007.

Morris, I. "The Athenian Economy Twenty Years after *The Ancient Economy.*" *Classical Philology* 89 (1994): 351–66.

———, ed. *Classical Greece: Ancient Histories and Modern Archaeology.* Cambridge, 1994.

———. "Archaeology and Archaic Greek History." In *Archaic Greece: New Approaches and New Evidence,* edited by N. Fisher and H. van Wees, 1–91. London, 1998.

Murray, O., and S. Price, eds. *The Greek City from Homer to Alexander.* Oxford, 1990.

Oliver, G. J. *War, Food, and Politics in Early Hellenistic Athens.* Oxford, 2007.

Osborne, R. *Classical Landscape with Figures: The Ancient Greek City and Its Countryside.* London, 1987.

———. "Social and Economic Implications of the Leasing of Land and Property in Classical and Hellenistic Greece." *Chiron* 18 (1988): 279–329.

———. "Greek Archaeology: A Survey of Recent Work." *American Journal of Archaeology* 108 (2004): 87–102.

Pleket, H. W. "Urban Elites and the Economy in the Greek Cities of the Roman Empire." *Münstersche Beiträge zur Antiken Handelsgeschichte* 3 (1984): 3–36.

———. "Greek Epigraphy and Comparative Ancient History: Two Case Studies." *Epigraphica Anatolica* 12 (1988): 25–37.

———. "The Roman State and the Economy: The Case of Ephesus." In *Entretiens d'archéologie et d'histoire, 1: Les échanges dans l'Antiquité—Le rôle de l'Etat,* edited by J. Andreau, P. Briant, and R. Descat, 115–26. St.-Bertrand-de-Comminges, 1994.

———. "Economy and Urbanization: Was There an Impact of Empire in Asia Minor?" In *Asia Minor Studien, 50: Stadt und Stadtentwicklung in Kleinasien,* edited by E. Schwertheim and E. Winter, 85–95. Bonn, 2003.

Polanyi, K., C. Arensberg, and H. W. Pearson. *Trade and Market in the Early Empires: Economies in History and Theory.* Glencoe, 1957.

Price, S., and Nixon, L. "Ancient Greek Agricultural Terraces: Evidence from Texts and Archaeological Survey." *American Journal of Archaeology* 109 (2005): 665–94.

Reger, G. *Regionalism and Change in the Economy of Independent Delos, 314–167 B.C.* Berkeley and Los Angeles, 1994.

———. "Aspects of the Role of Merchants in the Political Life of the Hellenistic World." In *Mercanti e politica nel mondo antico,* edited by C. Zaccagnini, 165–97. Rome, 2003.

———. "The Economy." In *A Companion to the Hellenistic World,* edited by A. Erskine, 331–53. Oxford, 2003.

Rostovtseff, M. *The Social and Economic History of the Hellenistic World.* Oxford, 1941.

————. *The Social and Economic History of the Roman Empire.* Oxford, 1957.

Rousset, D. "La cité et son territoire dans la province d'Achaïe et la notion de 'Grèce romaine.'" *Annales HSS* 59 (2004): 363–83.

Salmon, J. "The Economic Role of the Greek City." *Greece and Rome* 46 (1999): 147–67.

Schaps, D. M. *The Invention of Coinage and the Monetization of Ancient Greece.* Ann Arbor, 2004.

Scheidel, W. "The Greek Demographic Expansion: Models and Comparisons." *Journal of Hellenic Studies* 123 (2003): 120–40.

————, and S. von Reden, eds. *The Ancient Economy.* Edinburgh, 2002.

————, I. Morris, and R. Saller (eds.). *The Cambridge Economic History of the Roman World*, parts I–IV. Cambridge, 2007.

Schiavone, A. *The End of the Past: Ancient Rome and the Modern West.* Translated by M. Schneider. Cambridge, Mass., 2000.

Shipley, D. G. J., and M.-H. Hansen. "The Polis and Federalism." In *The Cambridge Companion to the Hellenistic World,* edited by G. R. Bugh, 52–72. Cambridge, 2006.

Shipley, G. "Hidden Landscapes: Greek Field Survey Data and Hellenistic History." In *The Hellenistic World: New Perspectives,* edited by D. Ogden, 177–198. London, 2002.

Shipton, K. *Leasing and Lending: The Cash Economy in Fourth-Century Athens.* London, 2000.

Snodgrass, A. *Archaic Greece: The Age of Experiment.* London, 1980.

————. *An Archaeology of Greece: The Present State and Future Scope of a Discipline.* Berkeley and Los Angeles, 1987.

Stanfield, J. R. *The Economic Thought of Karl Polanyi: Lives and Livelihood.* New York, 1986.

Starr, C. G. "Economic and Social Conditions in the Greek World." In *The Cambridge Ancient Histor,* vol. III.3, *The Expansion of the Greek World, Eighth to Sixth Centuries B.C.,* 2nd ed., edited by J. Boardman and N. G. L. Hammond, 417–41. Cambridge, 1982.

Strubbe, J. H. M. "The *Sitonia* in the Cities of Asia Minor under the Principate." *Epigraphica Anatolica* 10 (1987): 45–81; and 13 (1989): 99–121.

Temin, P. "A Market Economy in the Early Roman Empire." *Journal of Roman Studies* 91 (2001): 169–81.

———. "The Labor Market of the Early Roman Empire." *Journal of Interdisciplinary History* 34 (2004): 513–38.

Thompson, W. E. "The Athenian Entrepreneur." *L'antiquite Classique* 51 (1982): 53–85.

Veyne, P. *Bread and Circuses: Historical Sociology and Political Pluralism.* Translated by Brian Pearce. London, 1990.

von Reden, S. "Money in the Ancient Economy: A Survey of Recent Research." *Klio* 84 (2002): 141–74.

Weber, M. *The Agrarian Sociology of Ancient Civilizations.* Translated by R. I. Frank. London, 1976.

Wells, B., ed. *Agriculture in Ancient Greece: Proceedings of the Seventh International Symposium at the Swedish Institute at Athens, 16–17 May, 1990.* Stockholm, 1992.

White, K. D. *Greek and Roman Technology.* London, 1984.

Whittaker, C. R. "Do Theories of the Ancient City Matter?" In *Urban Society in Roman Italy,* edited by T. J. Cornell and H. K. Lomas, 1–20. London, 1993. (Reprinted as chapter 9 in *Land, City and Trade in the Roman Empire.* Aldershot, 1993.)

Wilkins, J. M., and S. Hill. *Food in the Ancient World.* Oxford, 2006.

Wilson, J.-P. "The 'Illiterate Trader'?" *Bulletin of the Institute of Classical Studies* 42 (1997–98): 29–56.

INDEX

Text: 11/15 Granjon
Display: Granjon
Compositor: International Typesetting and Composition
Indexer: Roberta Engleman
Printer and binder: Maple-Vail Book Manufacturing Group